New Hampshire

IMPRESSIONS

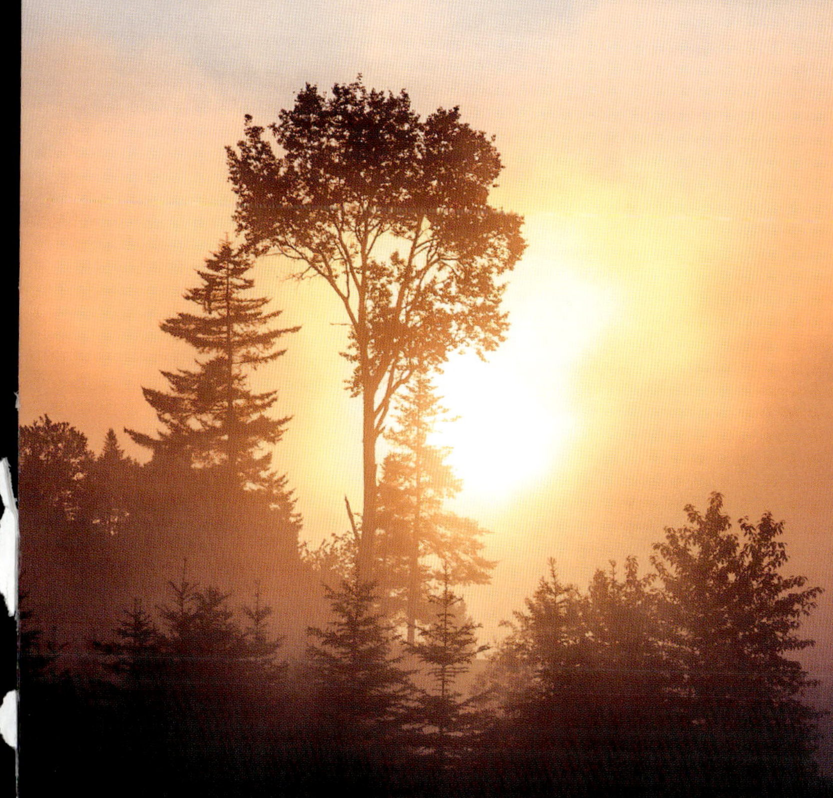

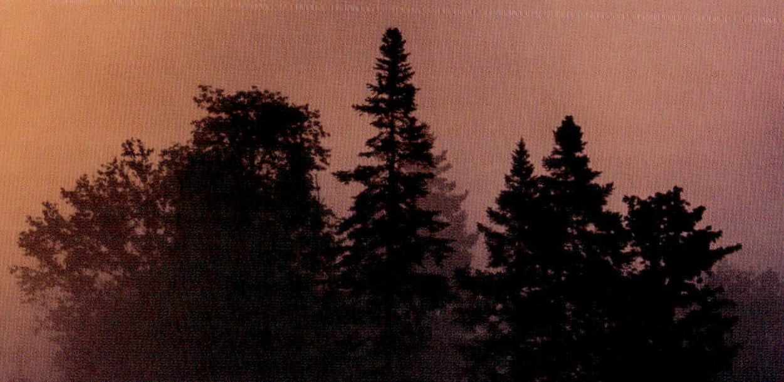

photography by William H. Johnson

FARCOUNTRY PRESS

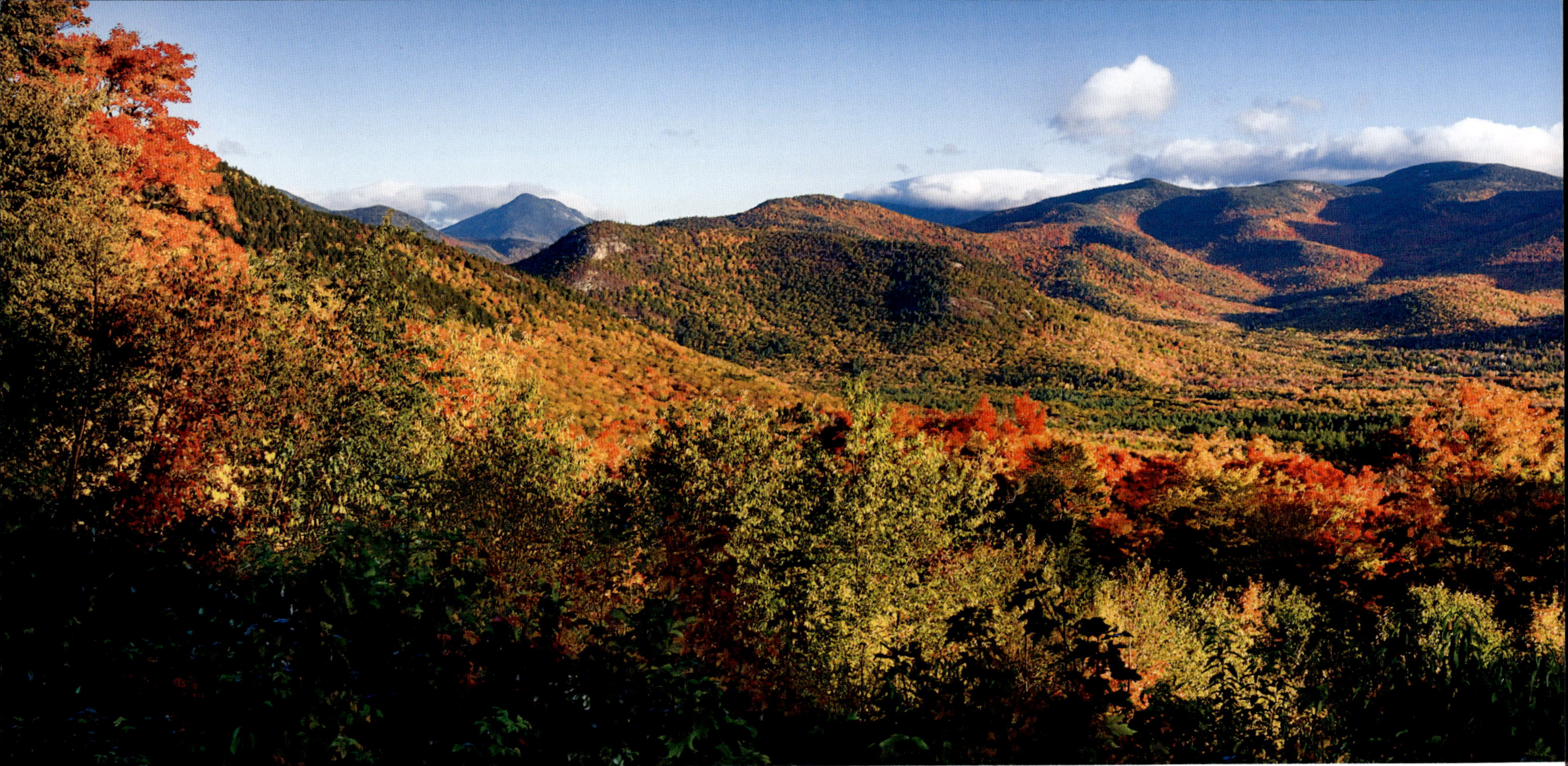

Above: Fall colors sweep the rugged North Country around Bartlett, located in the heart of the Mount Washington Valley.

Facing page: A red-spotted or eastern newt blazes a bright trail as an eft, the name for a juvenile terrestrial newt. The state amphibian, these newts help reduce insect populations and are hailed by New Hampshirites as a sign of spring.

Title page: Sunrise filters through rising fog at First Connecticut Lake in the Great North Woods. This series of lakes culminates in Fourth Connecticut Lake and the headwaters of the Connecticut River, which runs the length of New England and spills into Long Island Sound 400 miles to the south.

Front cover: Clouds drift across Squam Lake in the central Lakes Region. The state's second largest lake, Squam is home to a small population of nesting loons. Their eerie cries echo across the water.

Back cover: Twilight paints mountain ridgelines with color.

ISBN 10: 1-56037-595-7
ISBN 13: 978-1-56037-595-1

Text by Annie Graves

For more information about our books, write Farcountry Press, P.O. Box 5630, Helena, MT 59604; call (800) 821-3874; or visit www.farcountrypress.com.

Created, produced, and designed in the United States.
Printed in China.

18 17 16 15 14 1 2 3 4 5

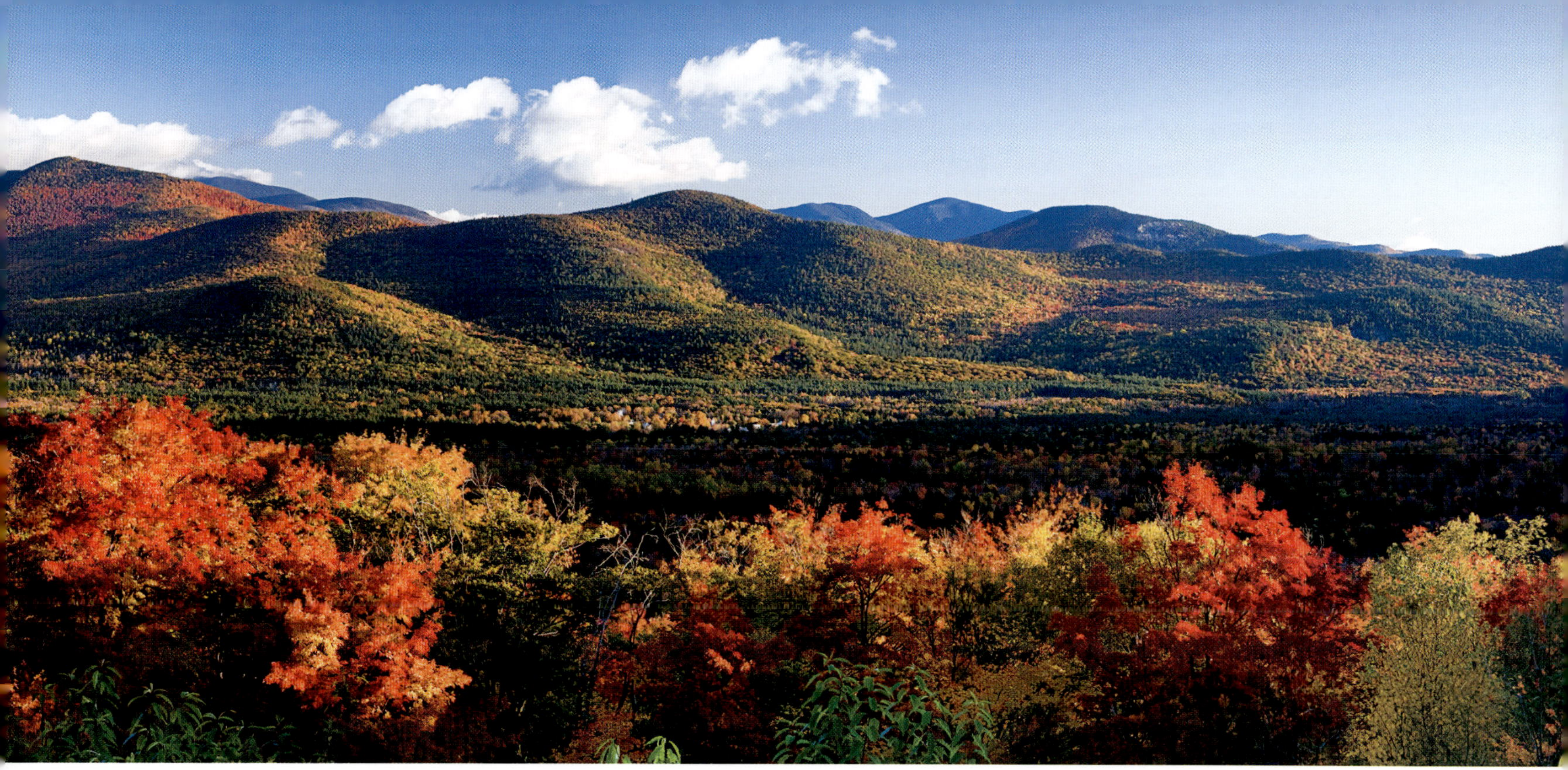

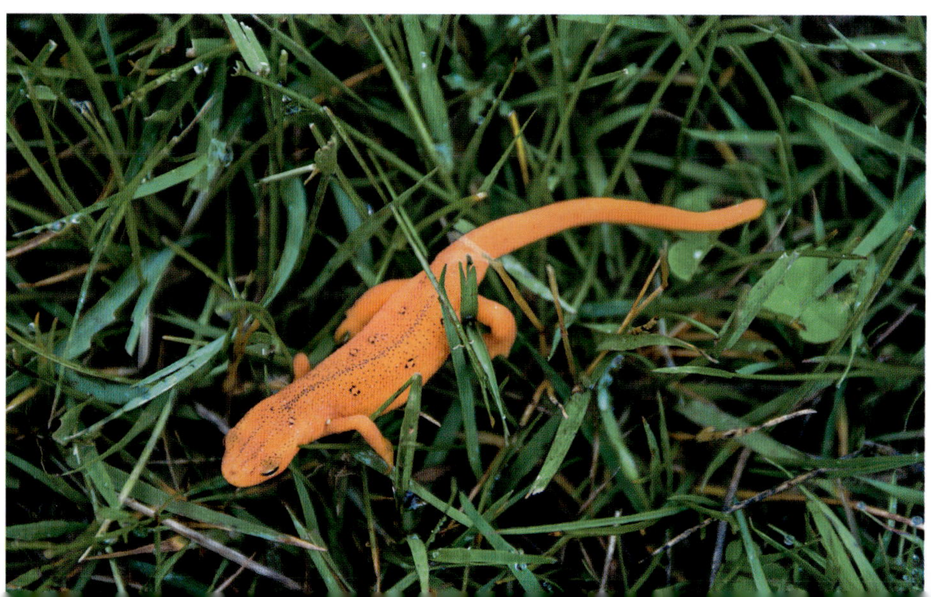

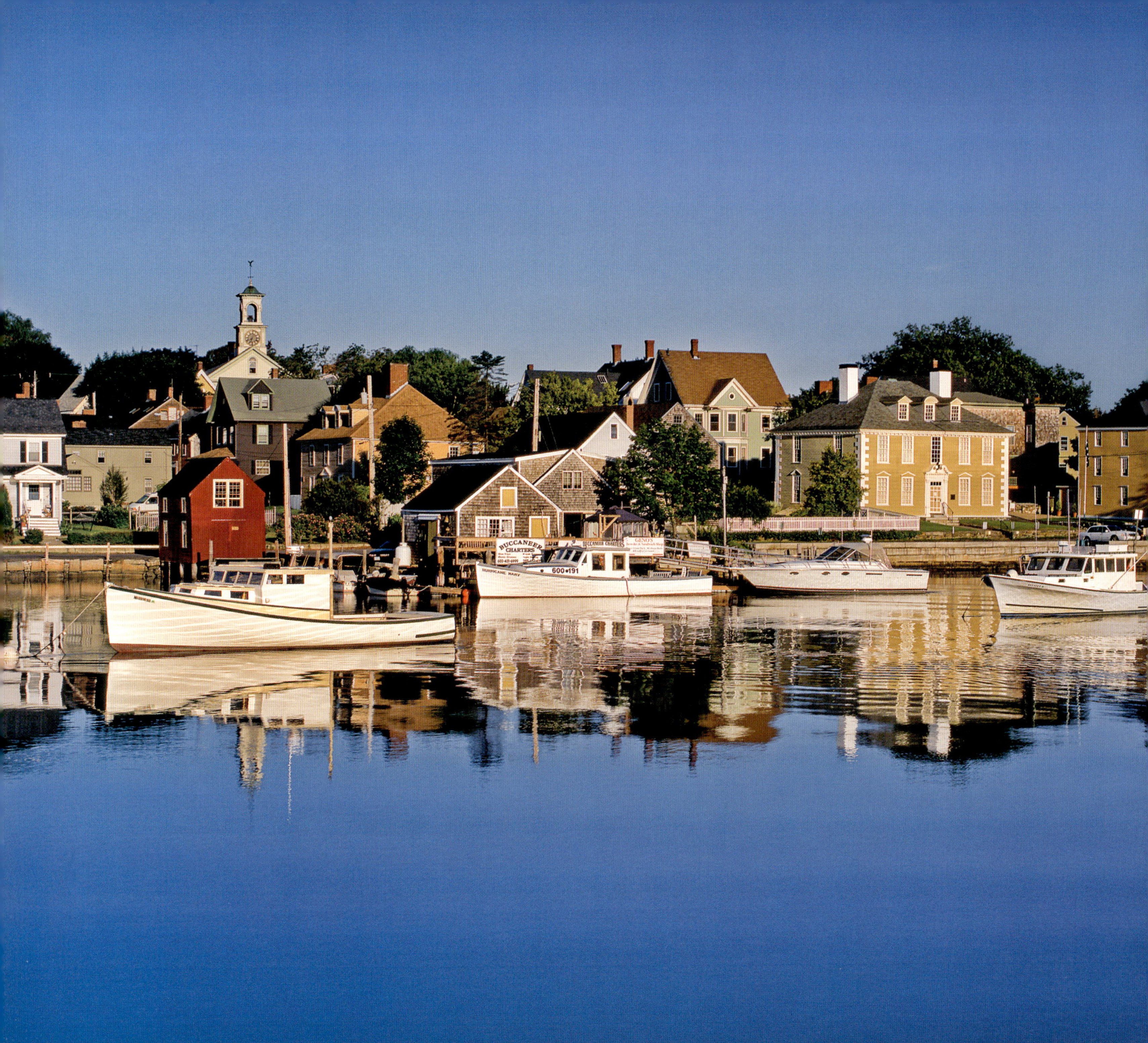
BUCCANEER CHARTERS
603-431-6999
BUCCANEER CHARTERS
GENO'S
HURRICANE MARY
600 191

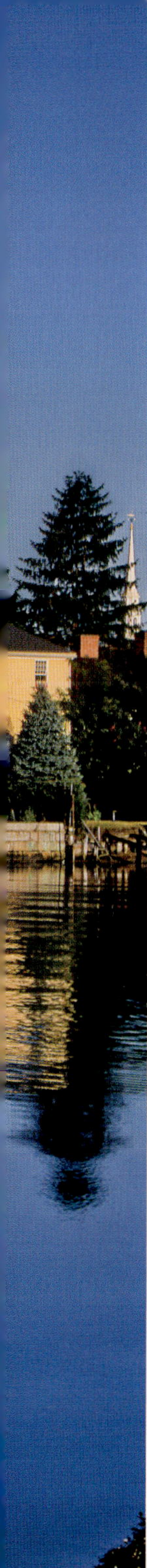

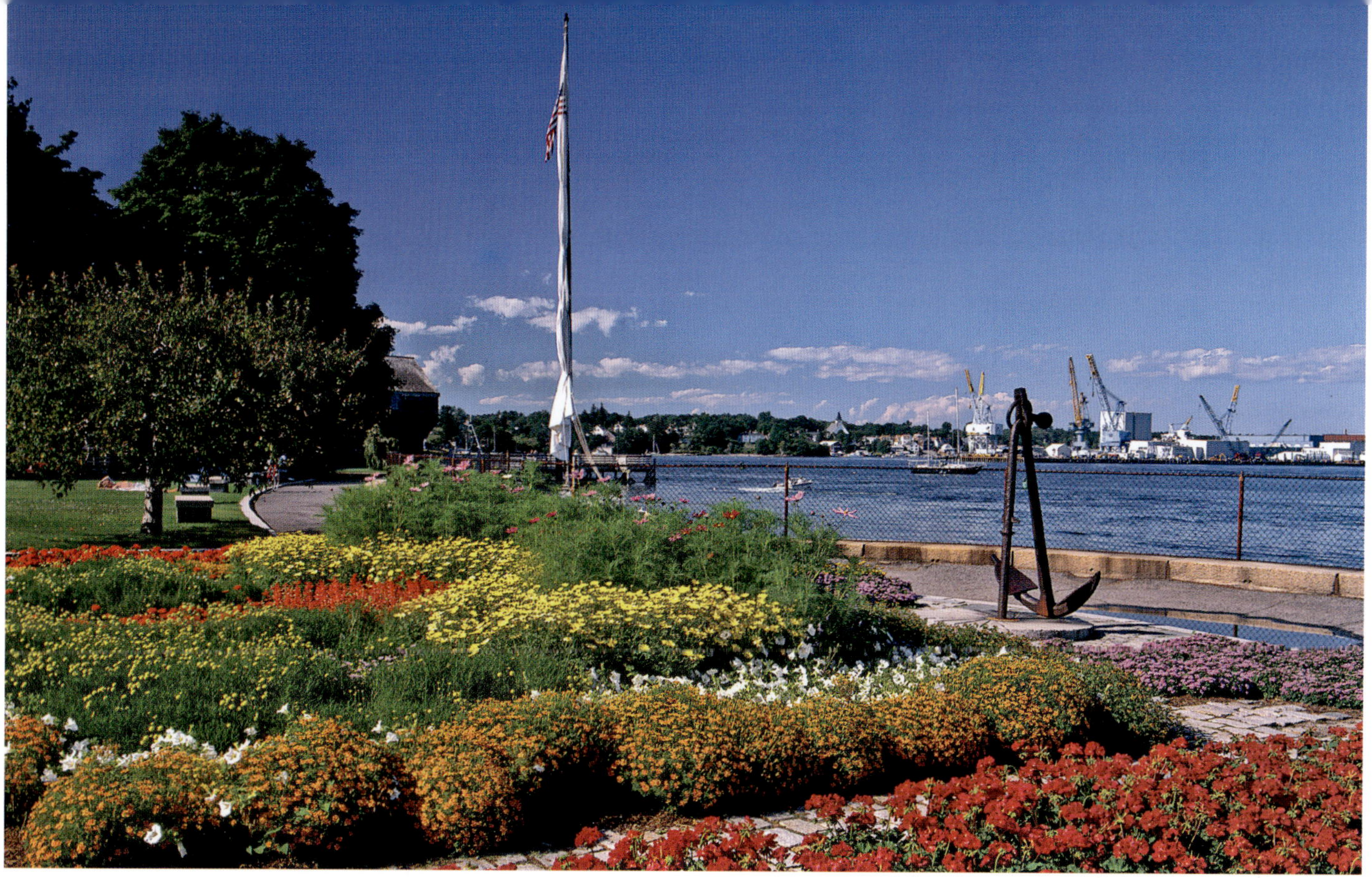

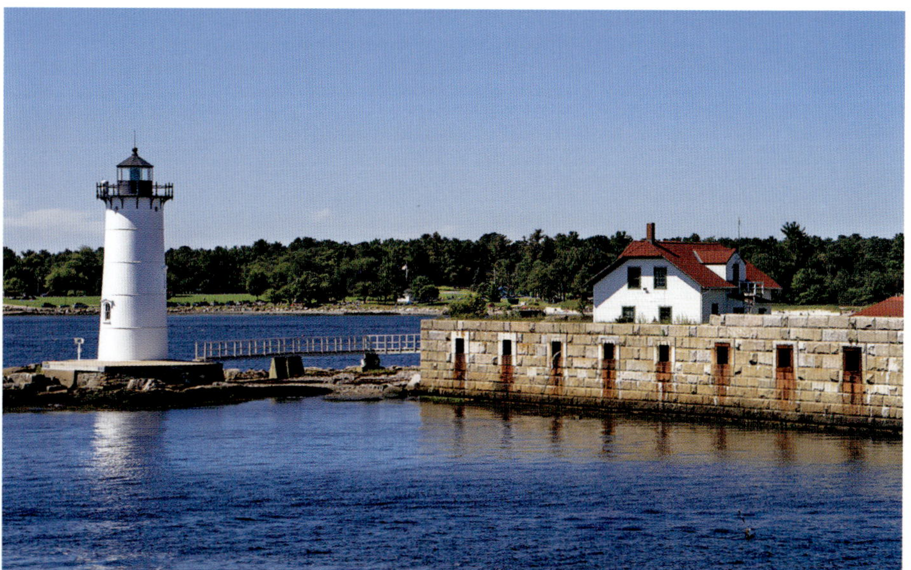

Above: In the historic seaport of Portsmouth, the deep harbor waters of the Piscataqua River roll up alongside Prescott Park, a lively venue for outdoor summer concerts, food festivals, theater performances, and film screenings.

Left: Picnickers at Fort Constitution State Historic Site on New Castle Island can enjoy views of Portsmouth Harbor Lighthouse and the ruins of Fort William and Mary, which was captured by revolutionaries in 1774.

Far left: A boat's-eye view of Portsmouth's waterfront hints at its architectural treasures. The settlement of Portsmouth dates back to the early 1600s.

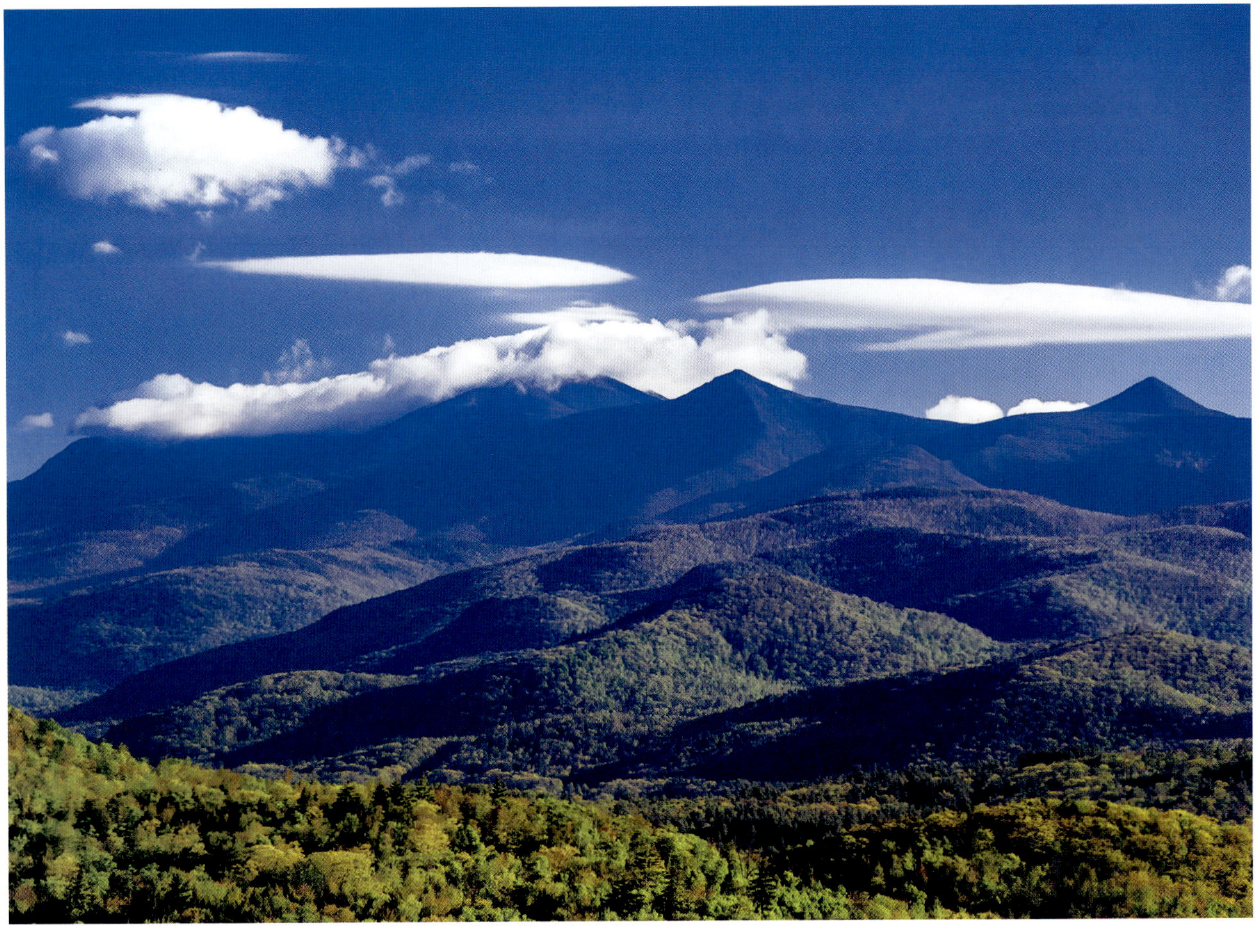

Above: Spring attracts avid hikers to the White Mountains. The Four Thousand Footer Club—mountains over 4,000 feet tall—has forty-eight members in the state, including Mt. Lafayette, 5,260 feet, shrouded in clouds; Mt. Lincoln, 5,089 feet, at right; and Mt. Liberty, 4,459 feet, far right.

Right: Atlantic waves pound a steady backbeat to the free concerts at the new Seashell Complex in Hampton Beach, a popular summer playground.

Far right: Unspoiled beauty is tucked just off the beaten path in small towns like South Brookline, just twenty-five miles south of New Hampshire's largest city, Manchester.

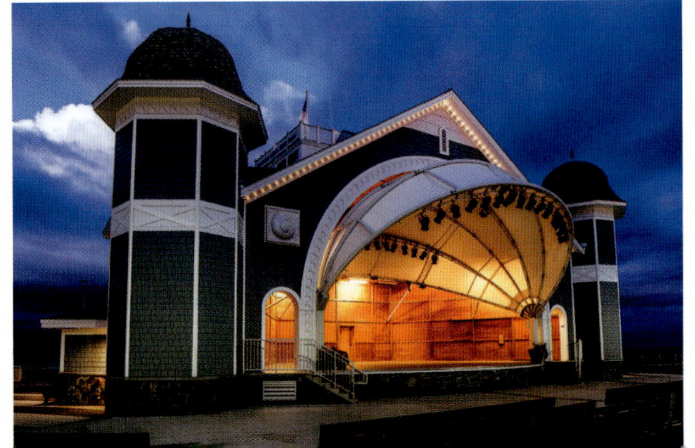

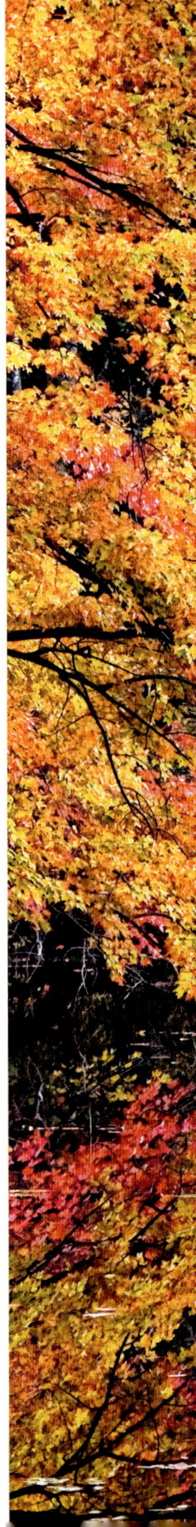

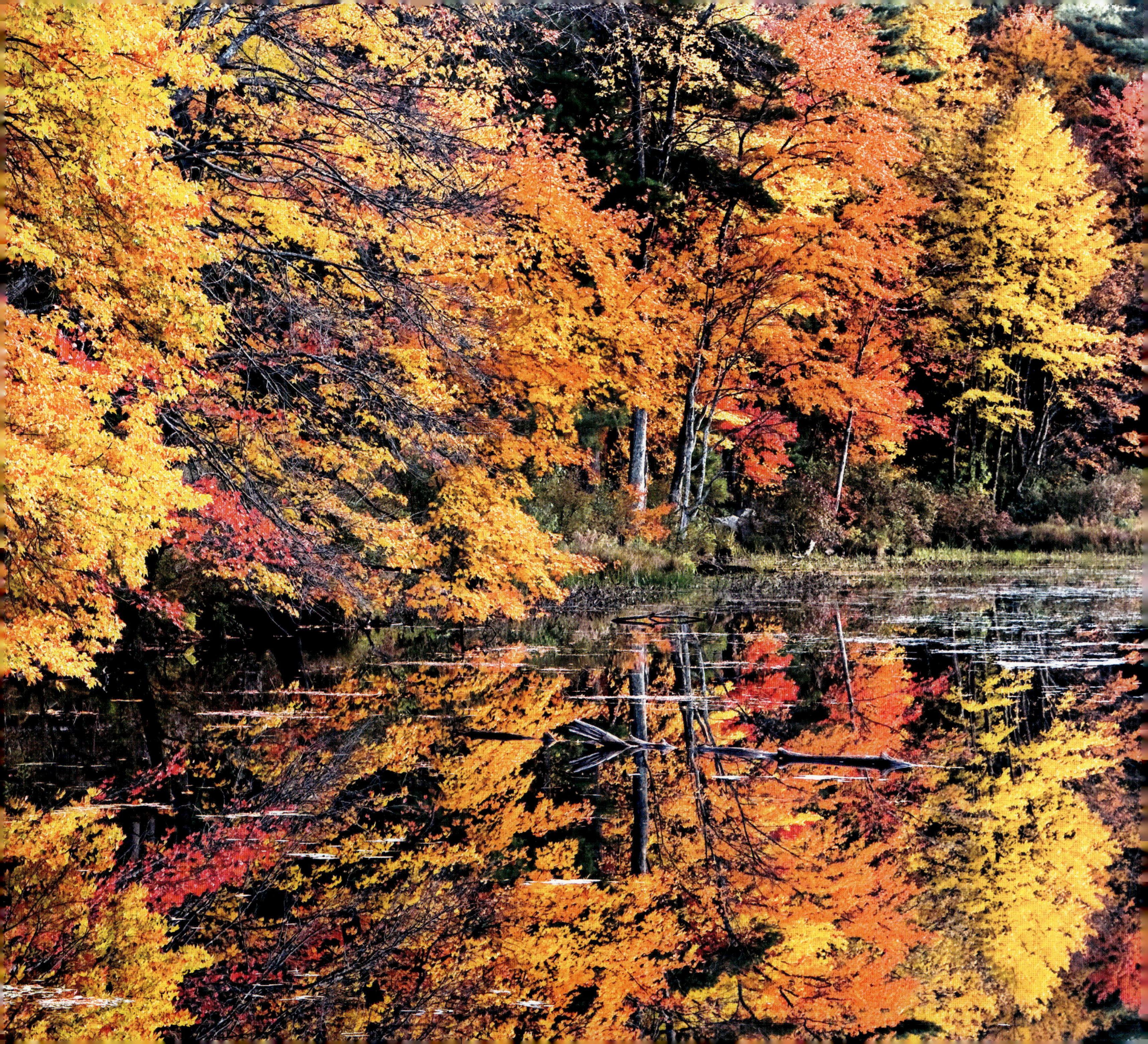

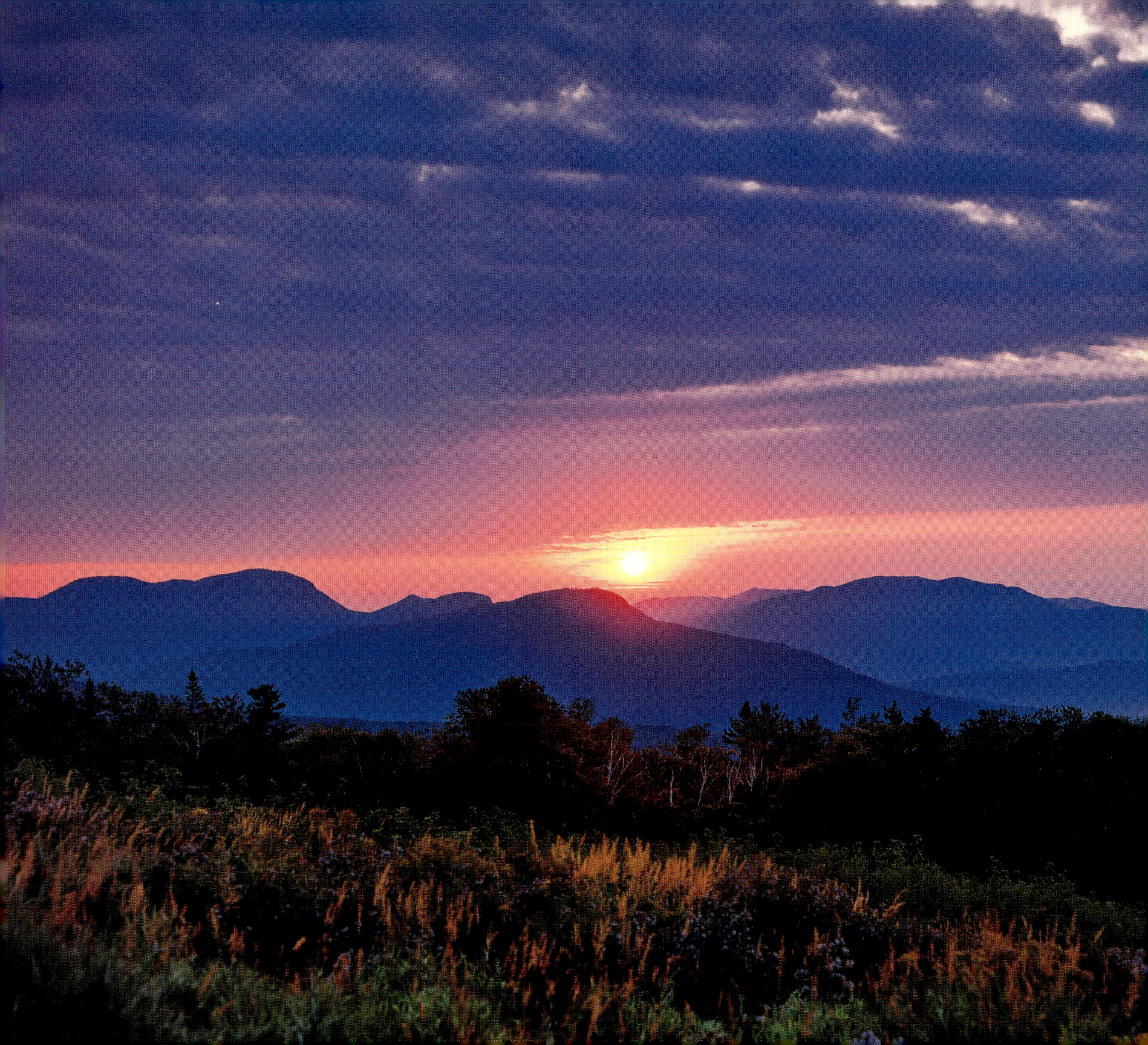

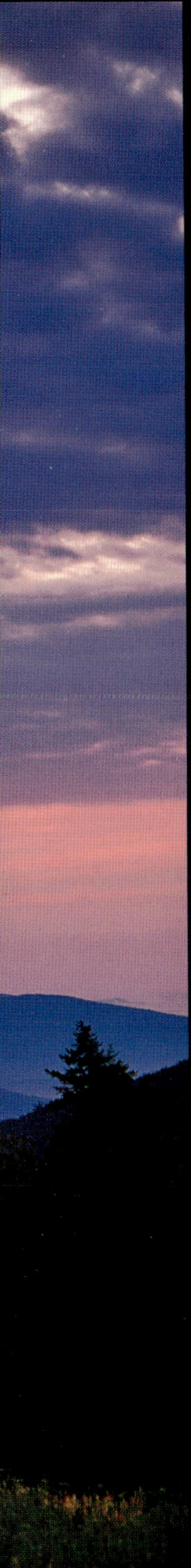

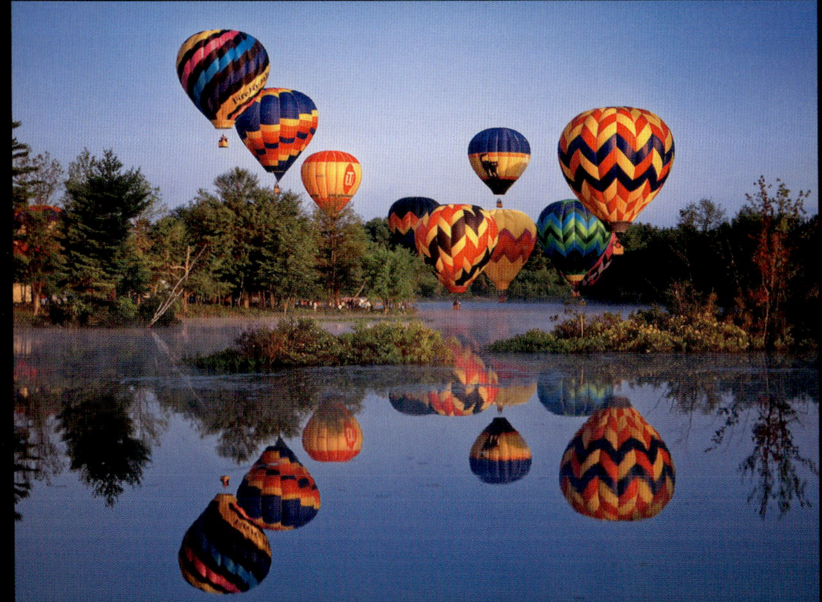

Left: Hot air balloons launch over the Suncook River at the Pittsfield Rotary Balloon Rally's annual festival, a summer tradition for more than thirty years.

Far left: The sun rises on Kancamagus Pass, which at almost 3,000 feet is the highest point of the Kancamagus Highway. Eye-popping vistas dot the thirty-four-mile scenic highway through the White Mountains.

Below: Dawn lights the fresh snowfall in the Lakes Region outside Belmont.

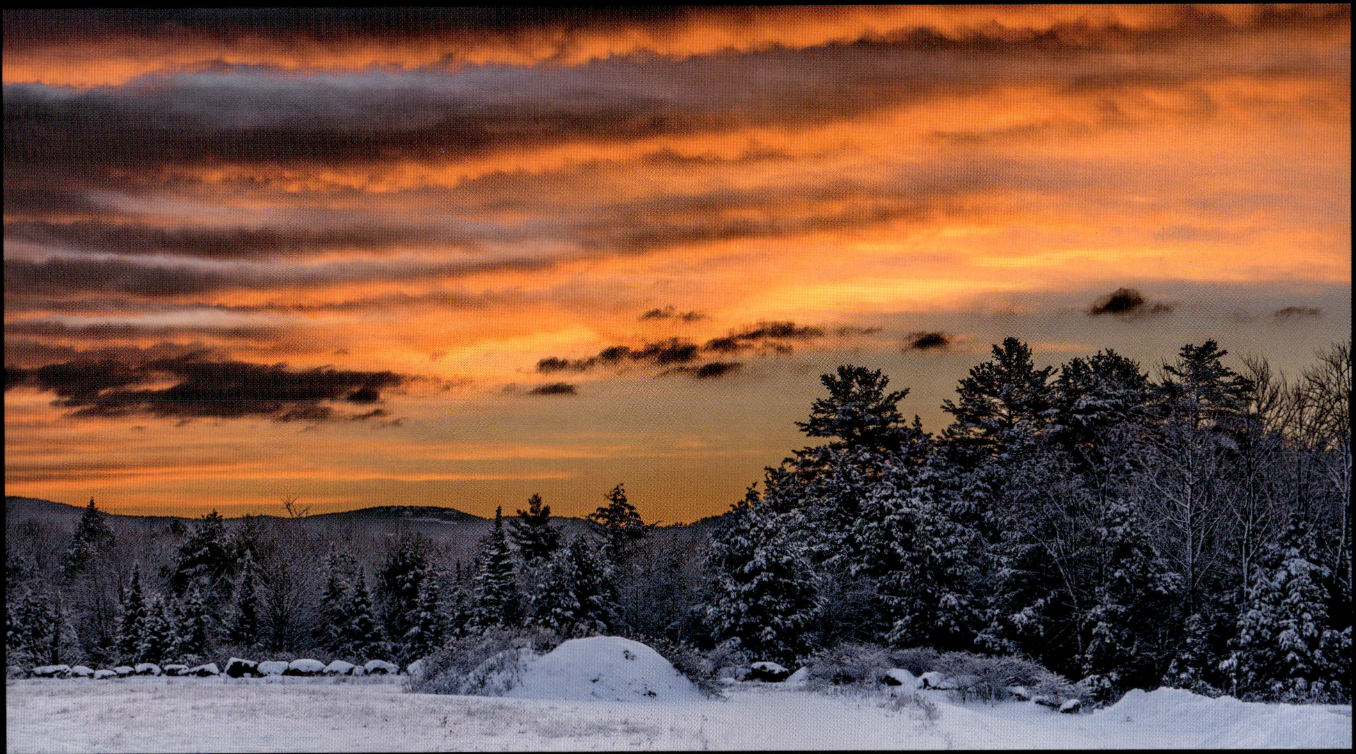

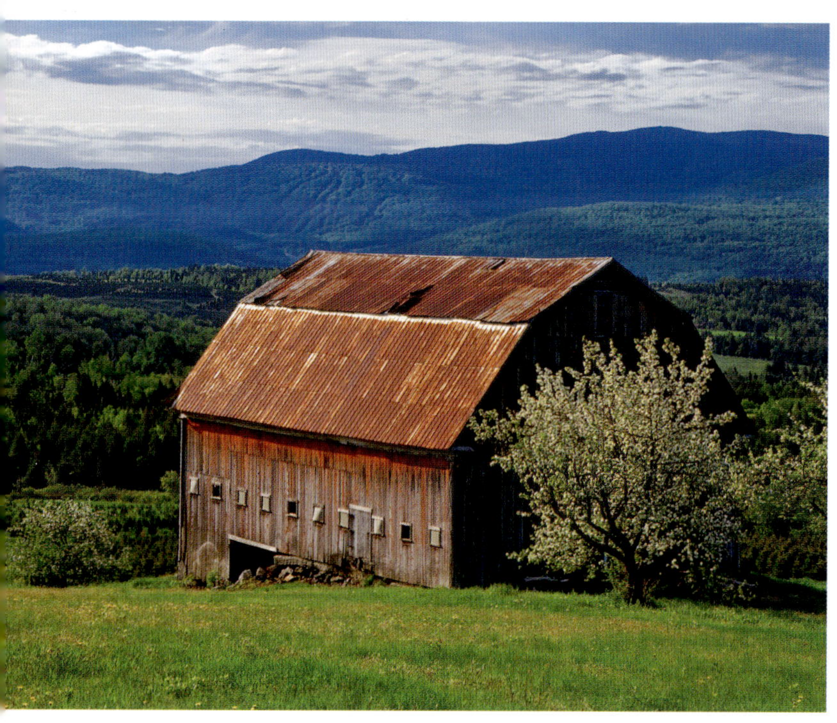

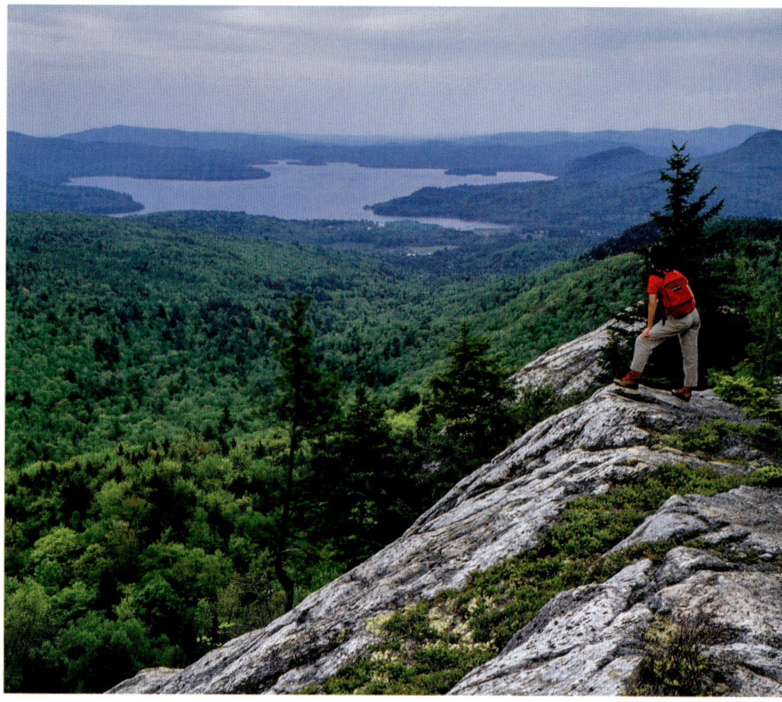

Above: A rustic barn looks toward Dixville Notch (both a mountain pass and a town), unmoved by the frenzy that erupts there every four years during national elections. The district's registered voters, usually fewer than twenty, cast the nation's first ballots just after midnight, and the polls close a few minutes later.

Above, right: A gift left by glaciers, spring-fed Newfound Lake, admired by a hiker on Bald Knob ledge, is famous locally for some of the cleanest water in the state. Cold and deep, it has been called "New Hampshire's best kept secret."

Facing page: In spring, Keene's lovely Central Square at the top of Main Street is enlivened with flowering crabapple trees and azalea bushes, presided over by an 1871 monument to Civil War veterans. A lively college town populated by restaurants and shops, Keene is also the business center of the Monadnock Region.

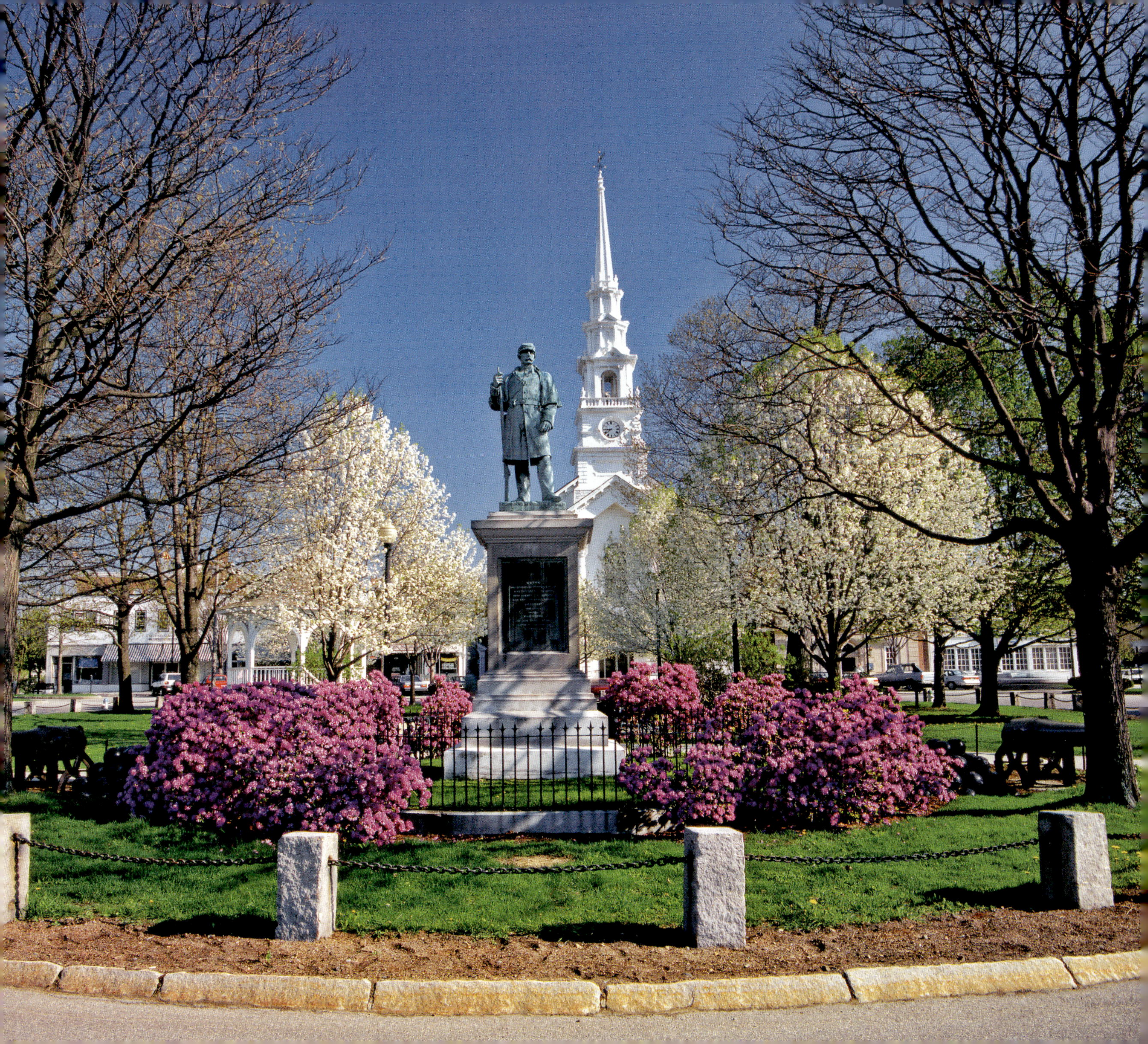

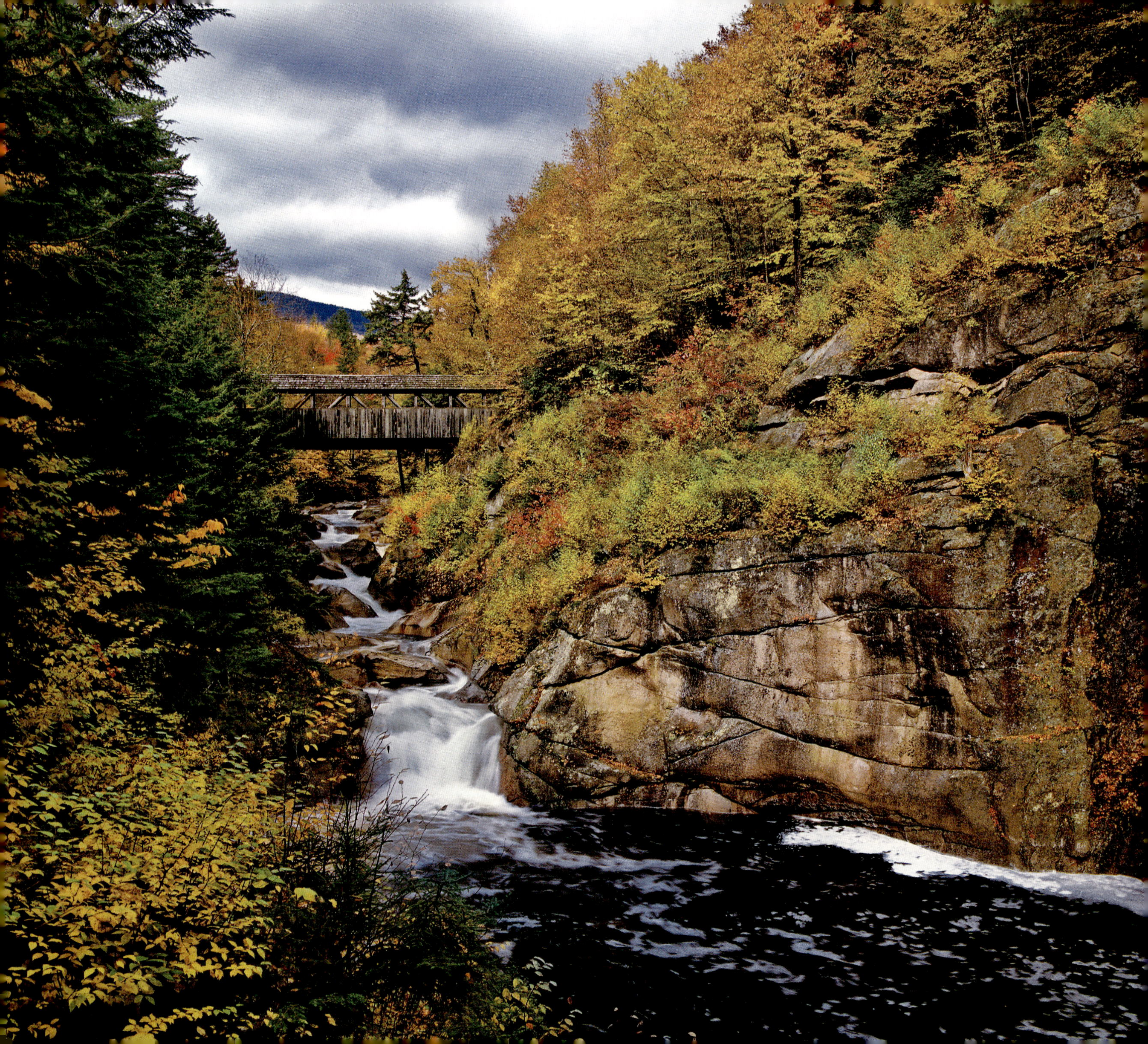

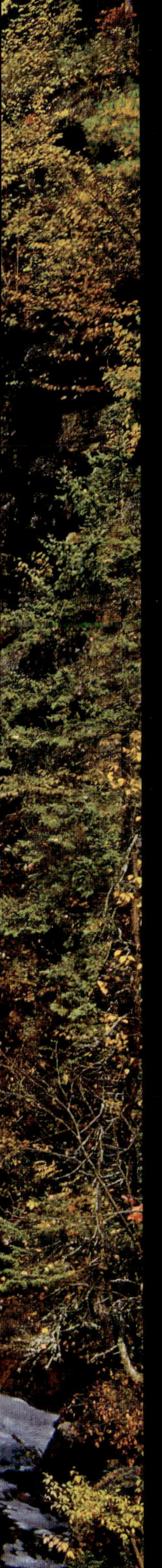

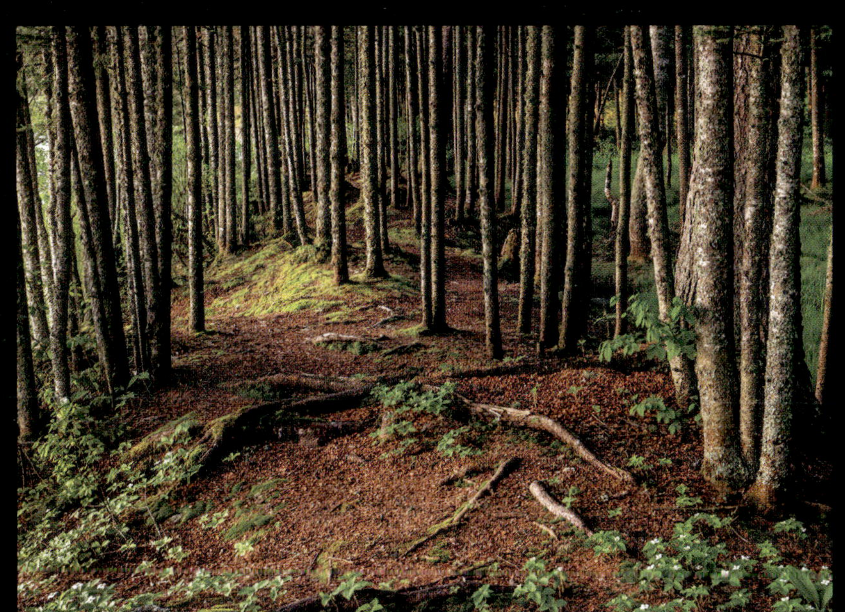

Left: Young tree trunks rise like tent poles at Coleman State Park on the shores of Little Diamond Pond in the remote North Country.

Far left: The Sentinel Pine Covered Bridge crosses the Pemigewasset River, where famed alpine skier Bode Miller reportedly trained by running from rock to rock to perfect his balance and concentration.

Below: Magnificent moose, averaging 1,000 pounds each, have reestablished themselves in New Hampshire. The Granite State's ample forests and lakes provide the perfect habitat for these impressive creatures.

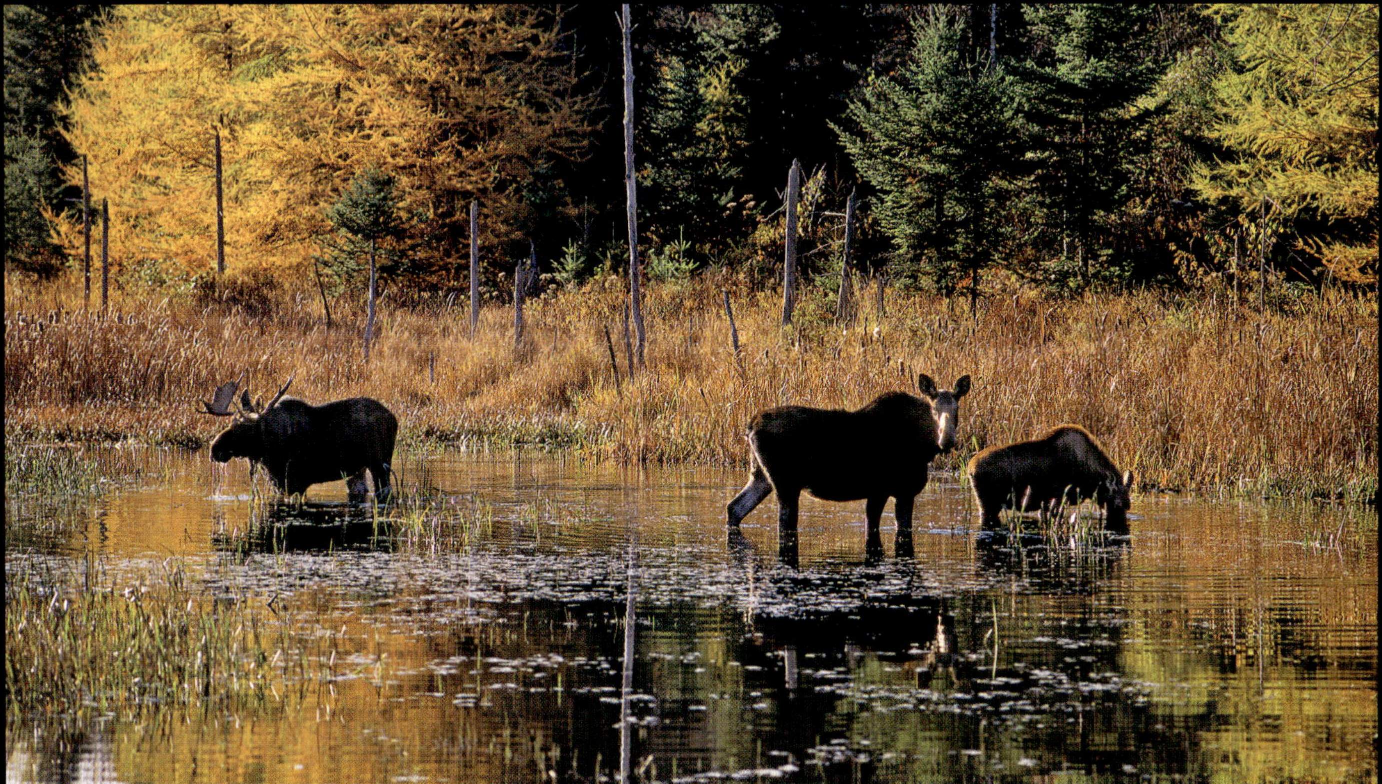

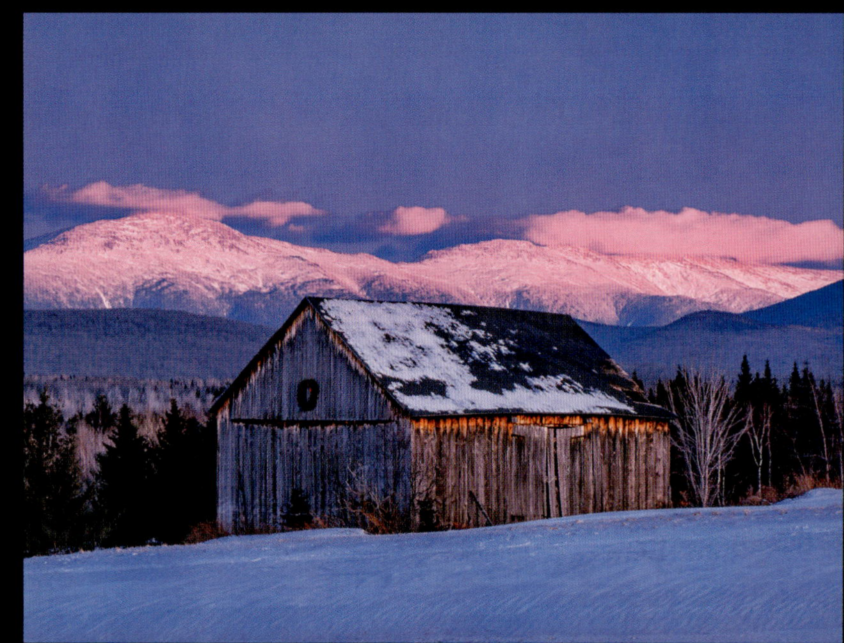

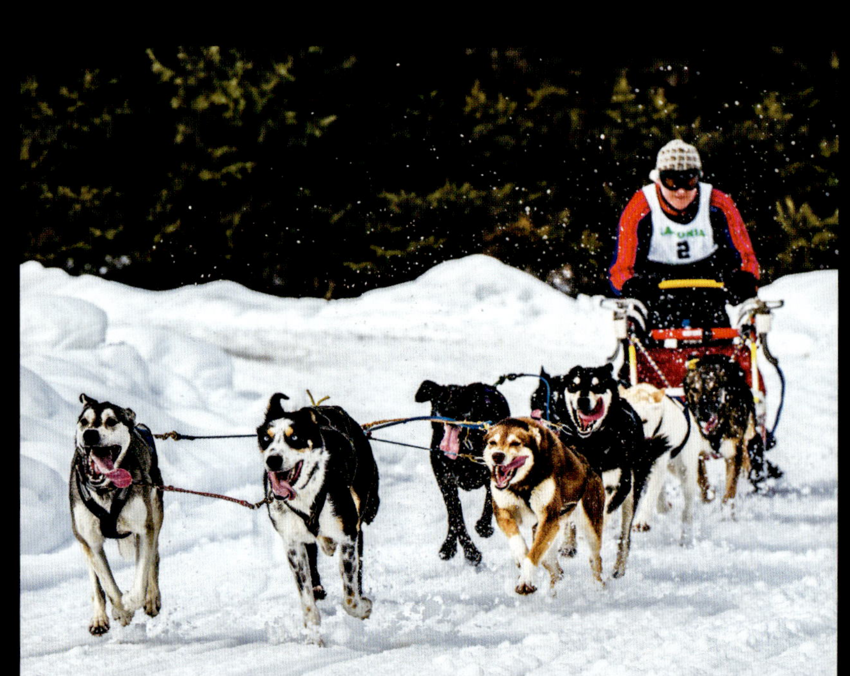

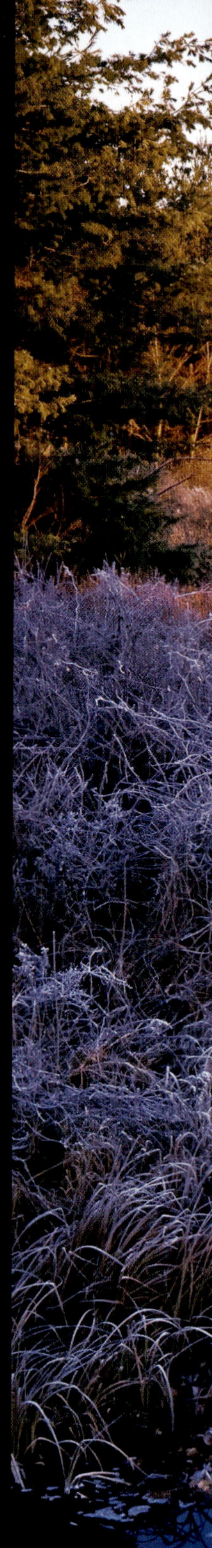

Above, right: Alpenglow bathes the White Mountains' Presidential Range, an illustrious group that includes Mounts Washington, Adams, Jefferson, and Monroe, in descending order of height.

Right: Snow flies as sled dogs from around the world chase the finish line in the Laconia World Championship Sled Dog Derby every February. The three-day event, begun in 1929, pits dogs and mushers against sixteen miles of rigorous terrain.

Far right: Perhaps famed local poet Donald Hall draws inspiration from the frosty alders and grasses at the edge of Kimpton Brook in the Dartmouth-Sunapee region. The Wilmott resident was the national Poet Laureate from 2006 to 2007, joining four other Poets Laureate from New Hampshire.

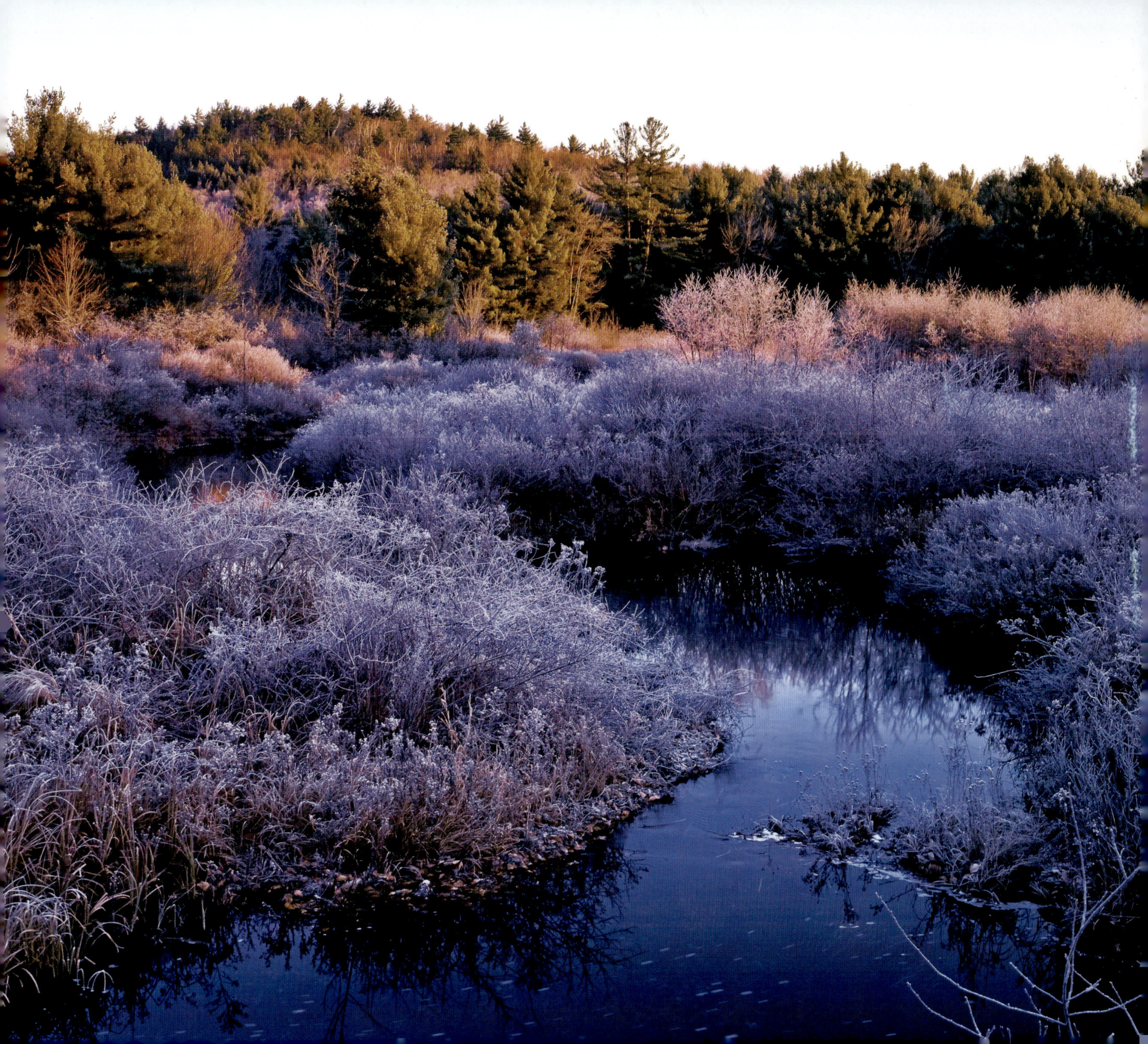

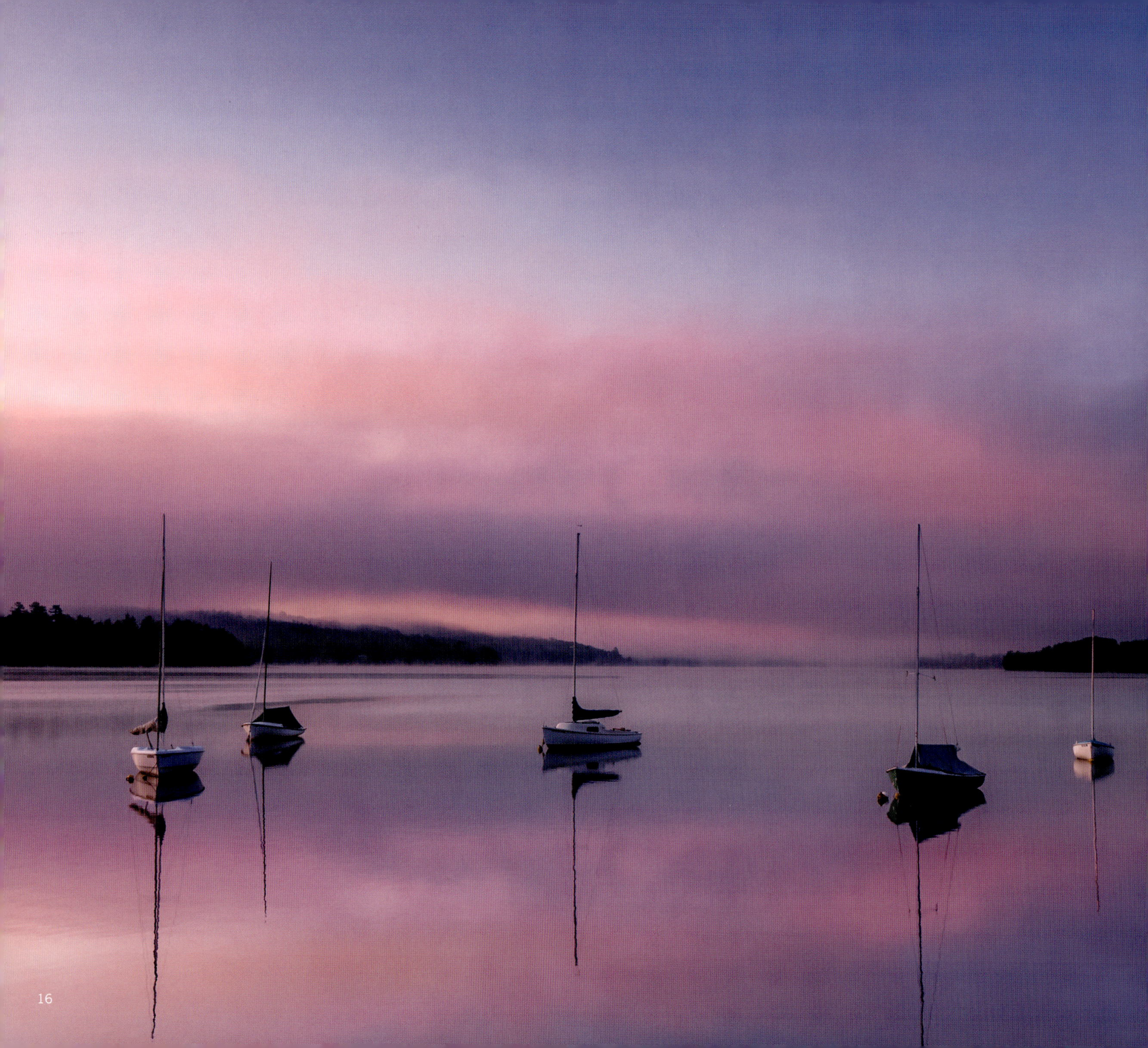

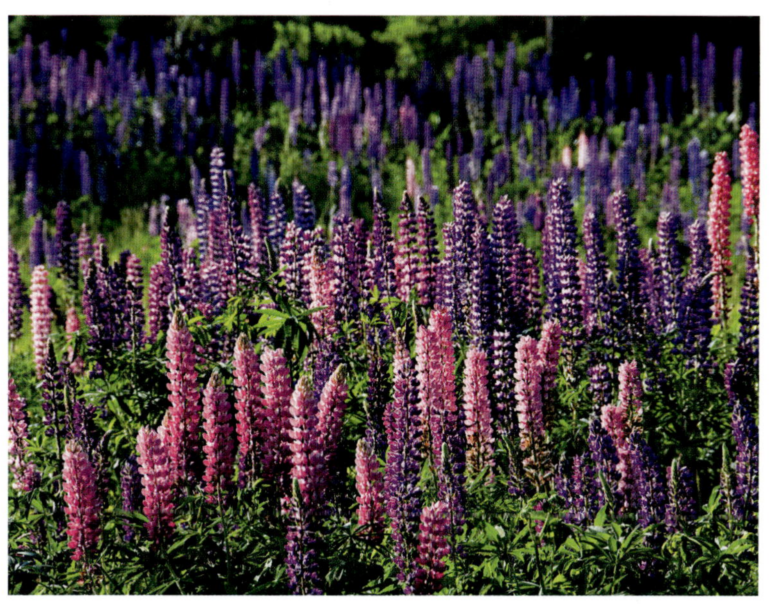

Left: In June, graceful lupines carpet the fields and hillsides. The beloved flower is celebrated by the Fields of Lupine Festival in Franconia Notch.

Far left: Dawn rubs the water at Mascoma Lake in Enfield as the fog lifts and sailboats wait silently. The Shaker community that settled by the lake in 1793 called this valley the "Chosen Vale."

Below: Colors run riot in spring, with dandelions leading the way, followed by pink and purple ground phlox and apple orchards bursting into bloom in the Merrimack Valley.

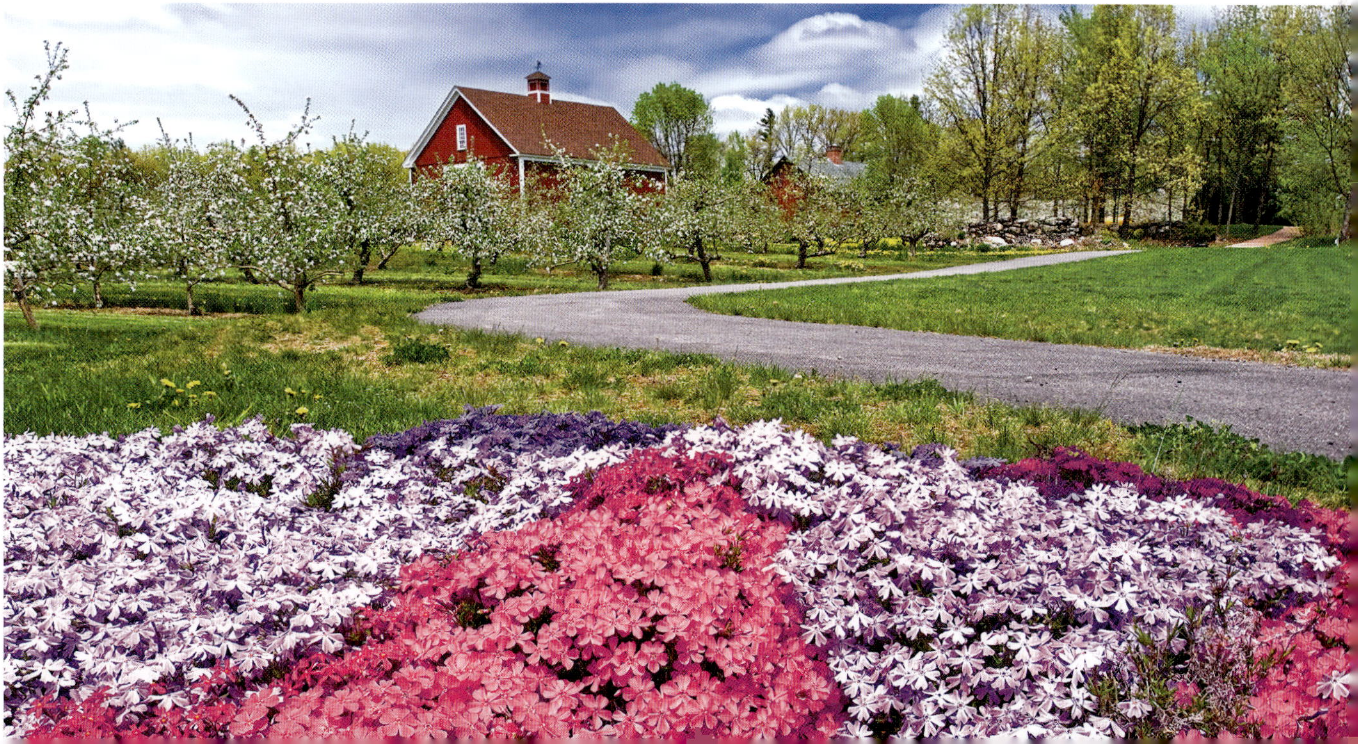

Facing page: Old-fashioned maple sap buckets are a sign of spring in Thornton, and in nearby White Mountain National Forest, golden treetops signal winter's slow retreat.

Right: Built in 1864, the charming Ashulot Covered Bridge is one of New Hampshire's fifty-four remaining covered bridges. It ranks as one of the state's most elaborate, and its Connecticut architect certainly thought the bridge was special: he patented the style.

Below right: Loon Mountain dons tartans and breaks out the bagpipes every fall for the New Hampshire Highland Games and Festival, the largest Scottish cultural fair in the Northeast. With dancing, piping, caber tossing, and sheep dog trials, the Games bring out the Scot in everyone.

Below: Founded in 1866 as a land-grant college, the University of New Hampshire now serves almost 15,000 students on its main campus in Durham. Its centerpiece, Thompson Hall, was constructed of local bricks and granite in 1893.

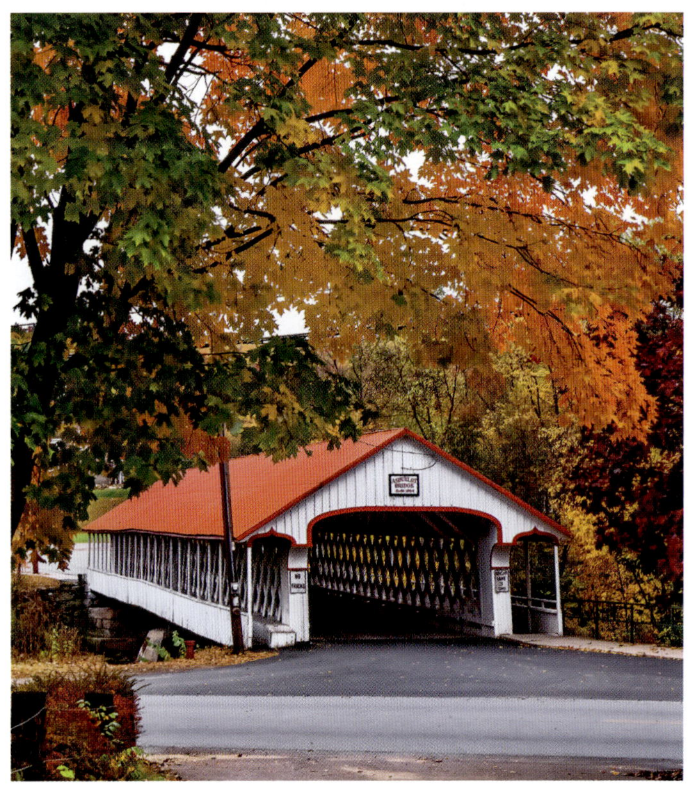

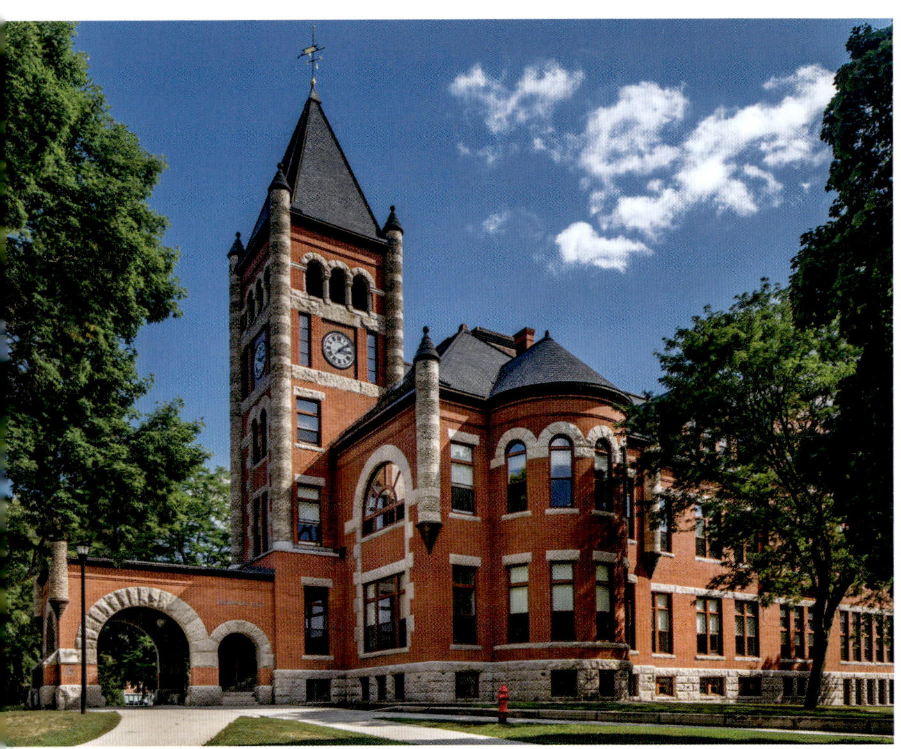

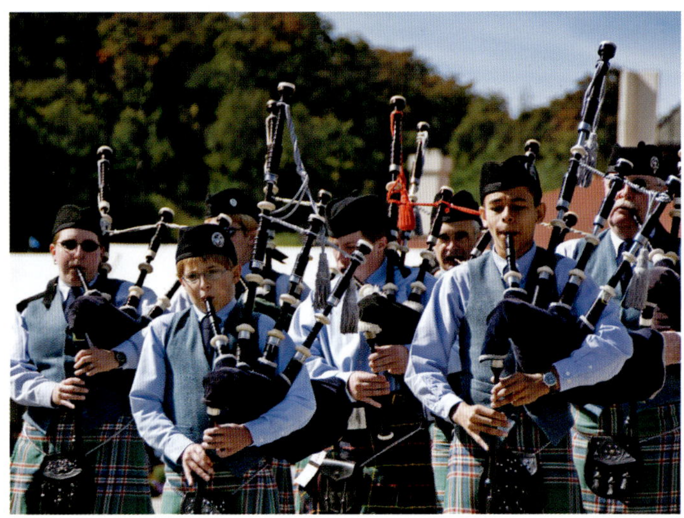

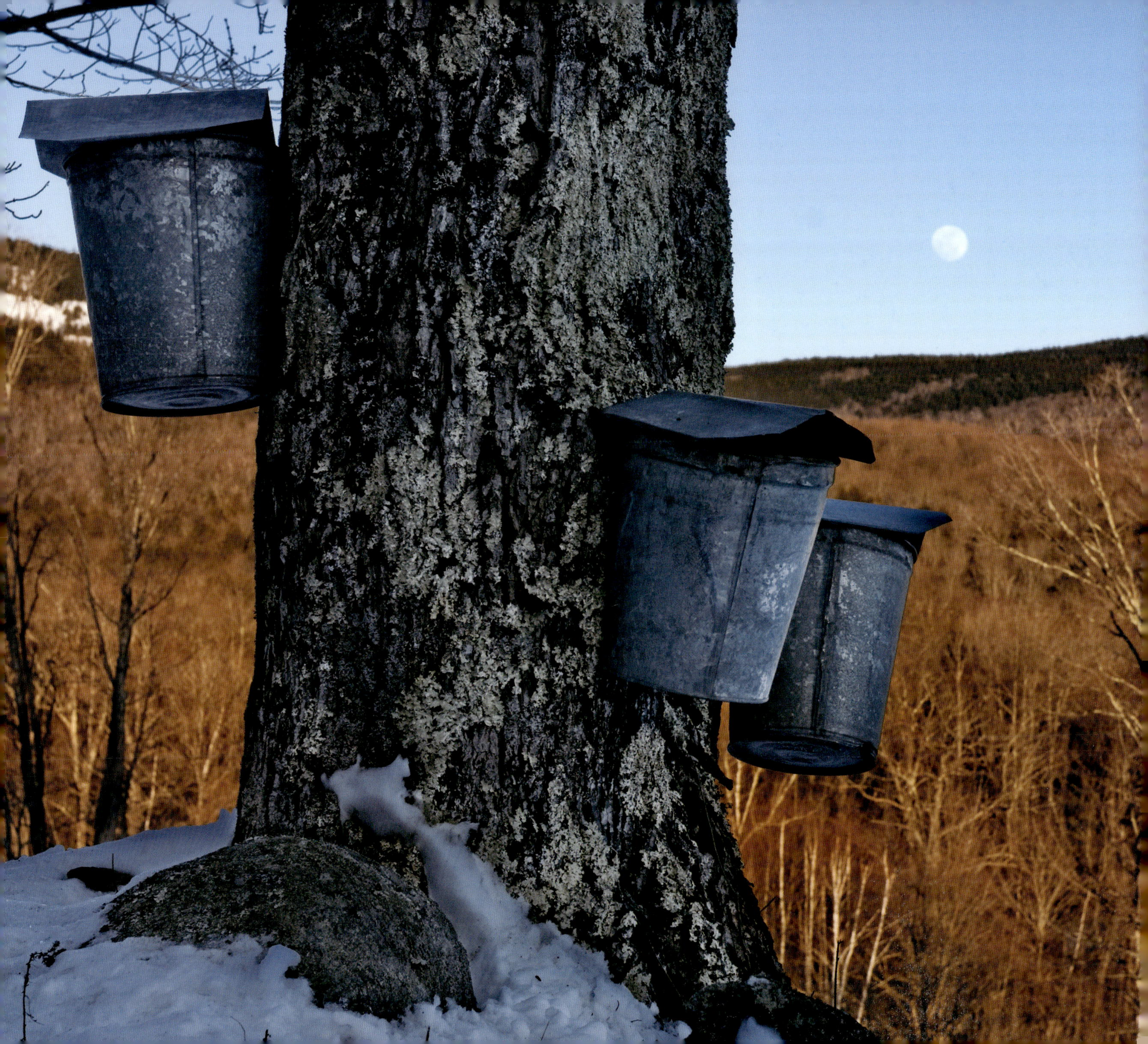

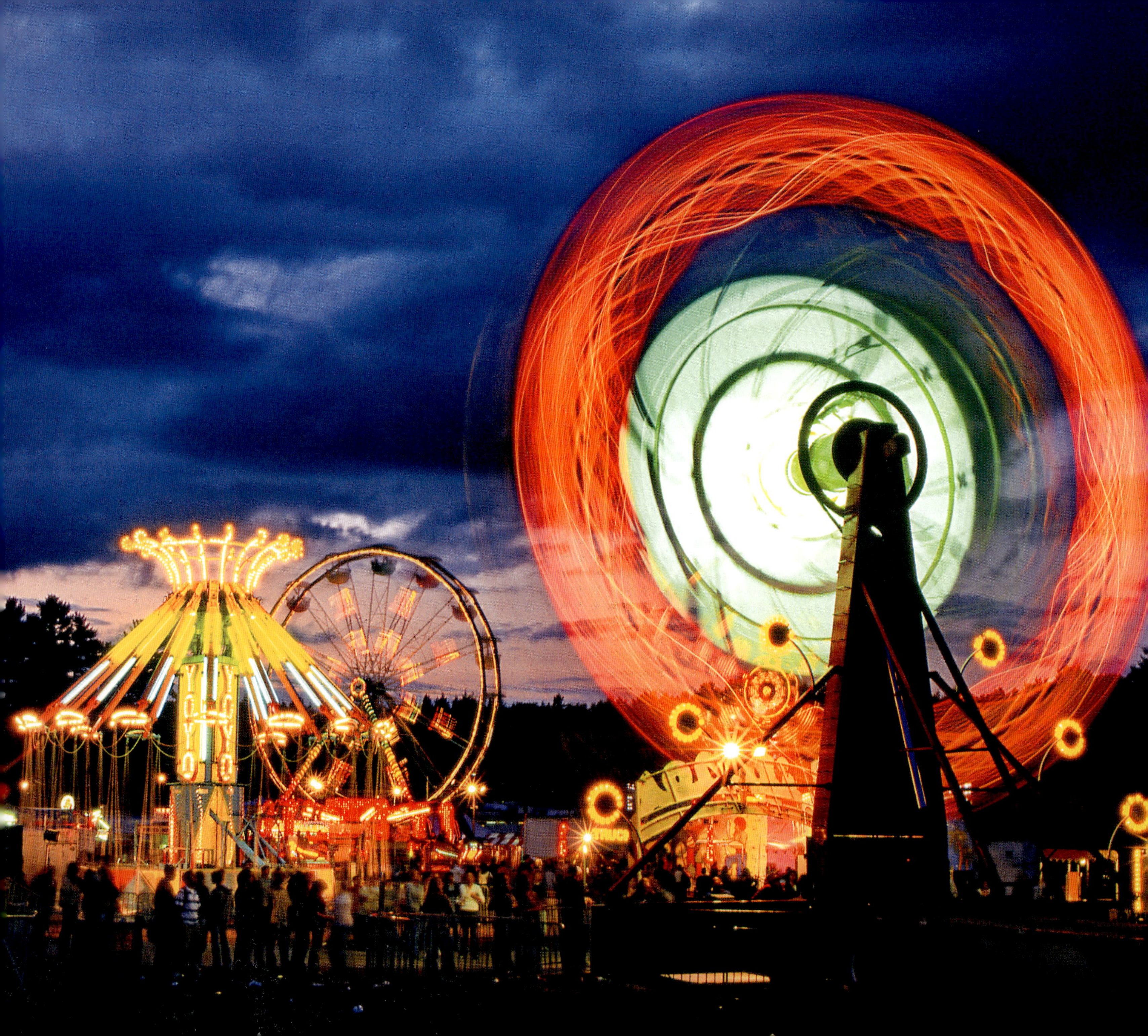
YOYO
YOYO

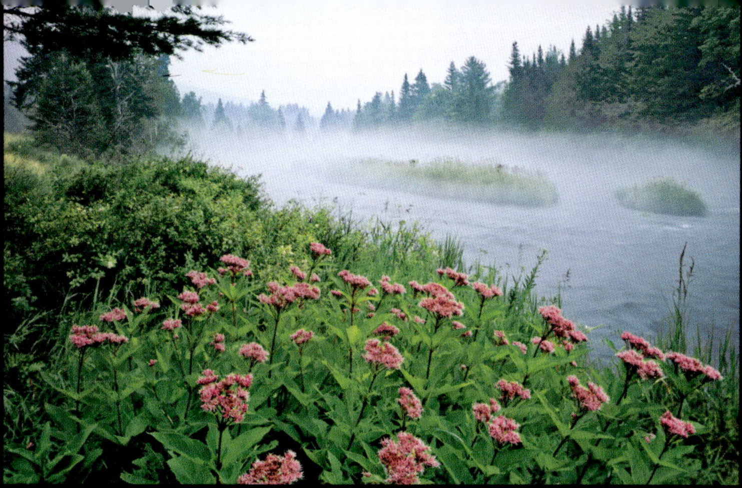

Left: Fog rises off the Connecticut River, deep in the Great North Woods in Pittsburg. Nestled next to the Canadian border, Pittsburg is a destination for wilderness enthusiasts, drawing avid fishermen, snowmobilers, and anyone looking to spot moose along Moose Alley.

Far left: The Deerfield Fair has been around since 1876, and with livestock shows, antique tractor pulls, and brightly lit amusement rides, there's much to see and do.

Below: Early morning sunrise strikes Lake Massabesic, the pristine water supply for the city of Manchester. Sailing, fishing, mountain biking, and trail running are favorite activities near this serene lake.

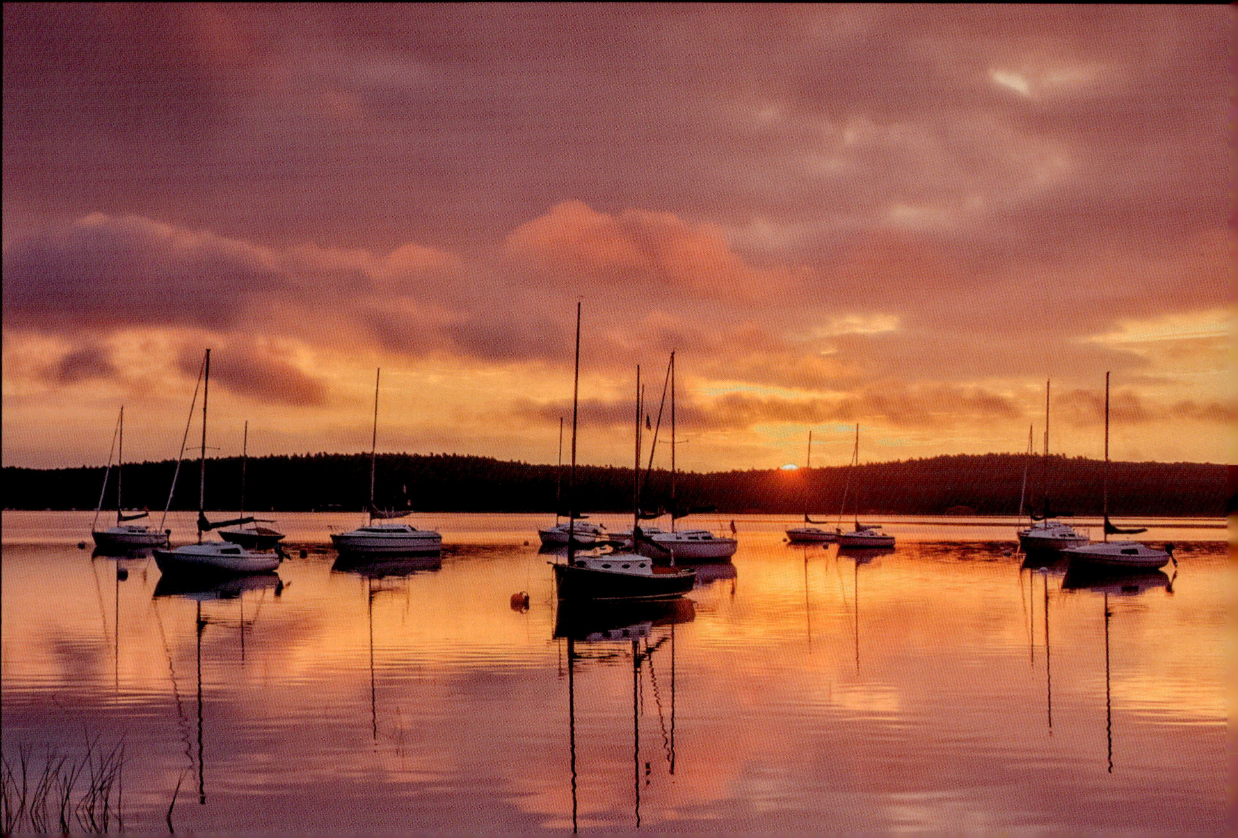

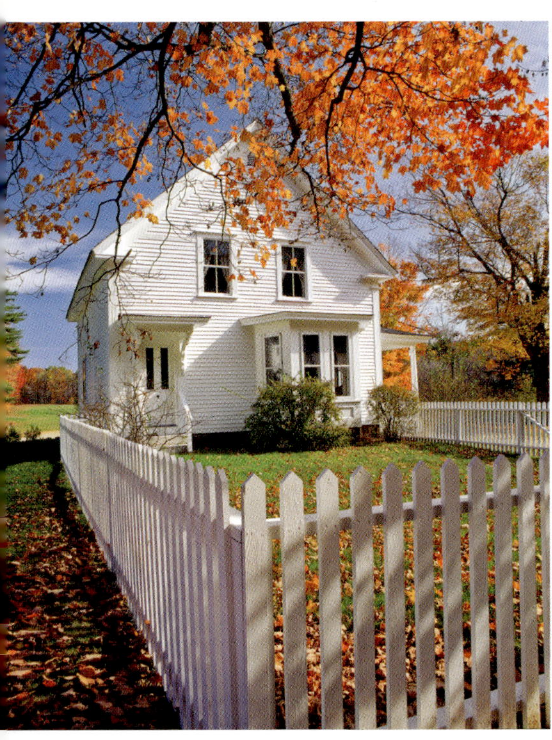

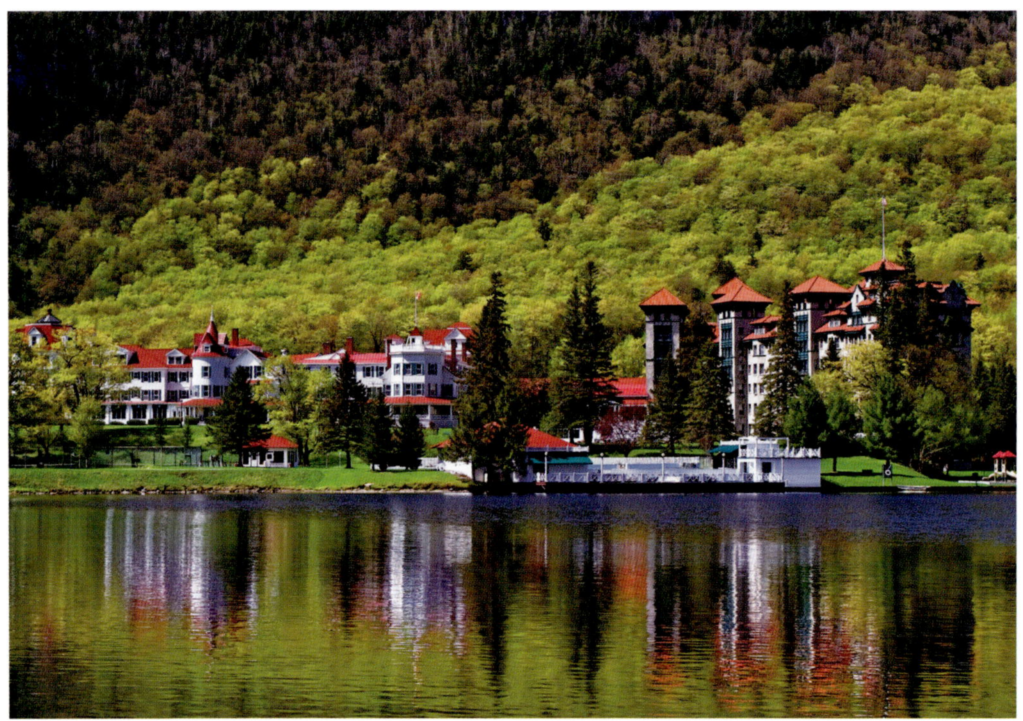

Above left: No ordinary farmhouse, The Robert Frost Farm in Derry was home to the revered Pulitzer Prize-winning poet from 1900 to 1911. Here, Frost wrote such classic poems as "The Death of the Hired Man."

Above right: Deep in the Great North Woods, surrounded by 15,000 acres of wilderness, tiny Dixville Notch is home to The Balsams Grand Resort Hotel, which opened in the late 1800s. Renovations to restore the grand resort began in 2011.

Facing page: Enjoy a perfect autumn stroll on Lovers Lane in Sugar Hill. The quiet of a New England fall draws thousands of travelers to New Hampshire every year.

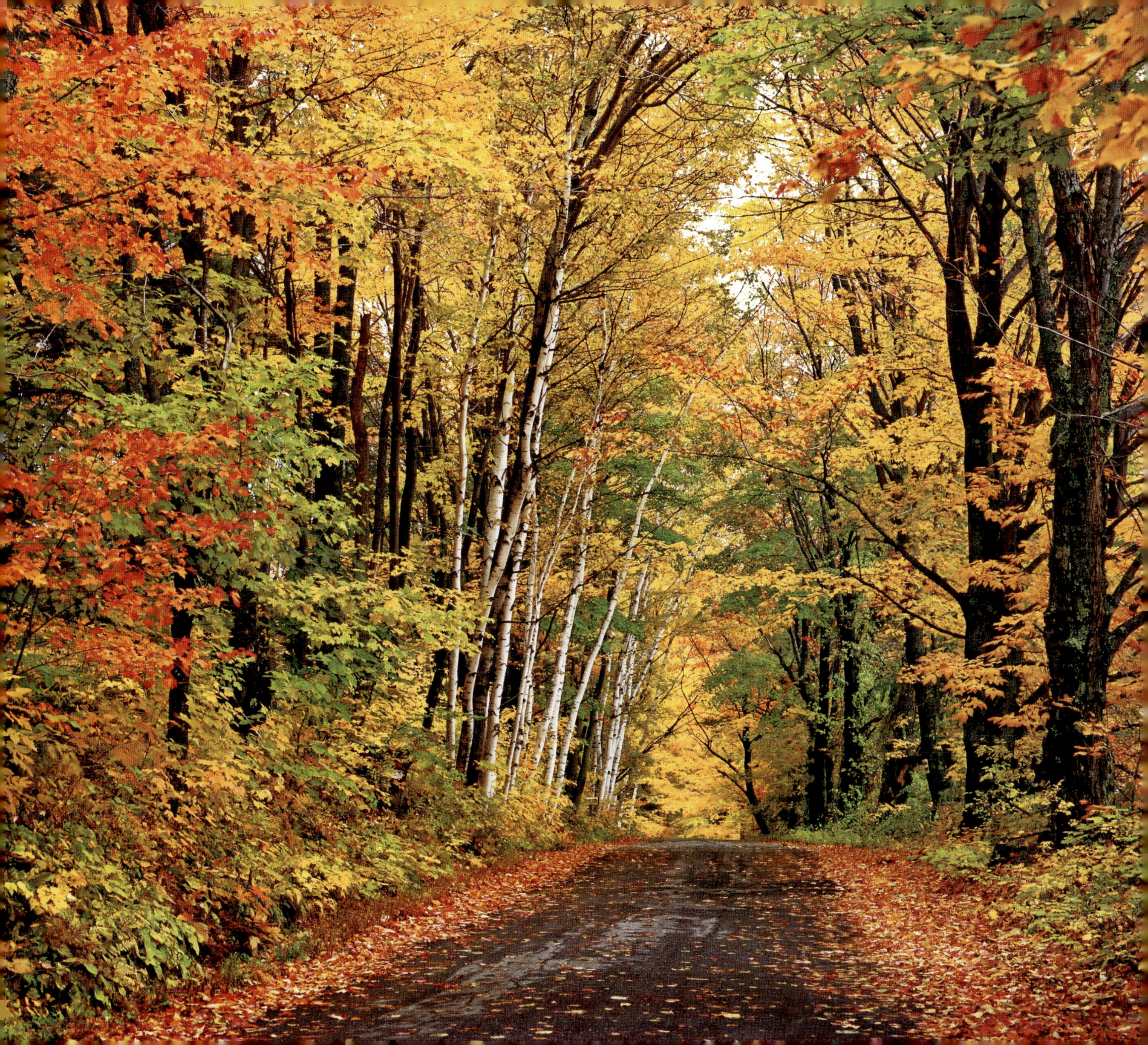

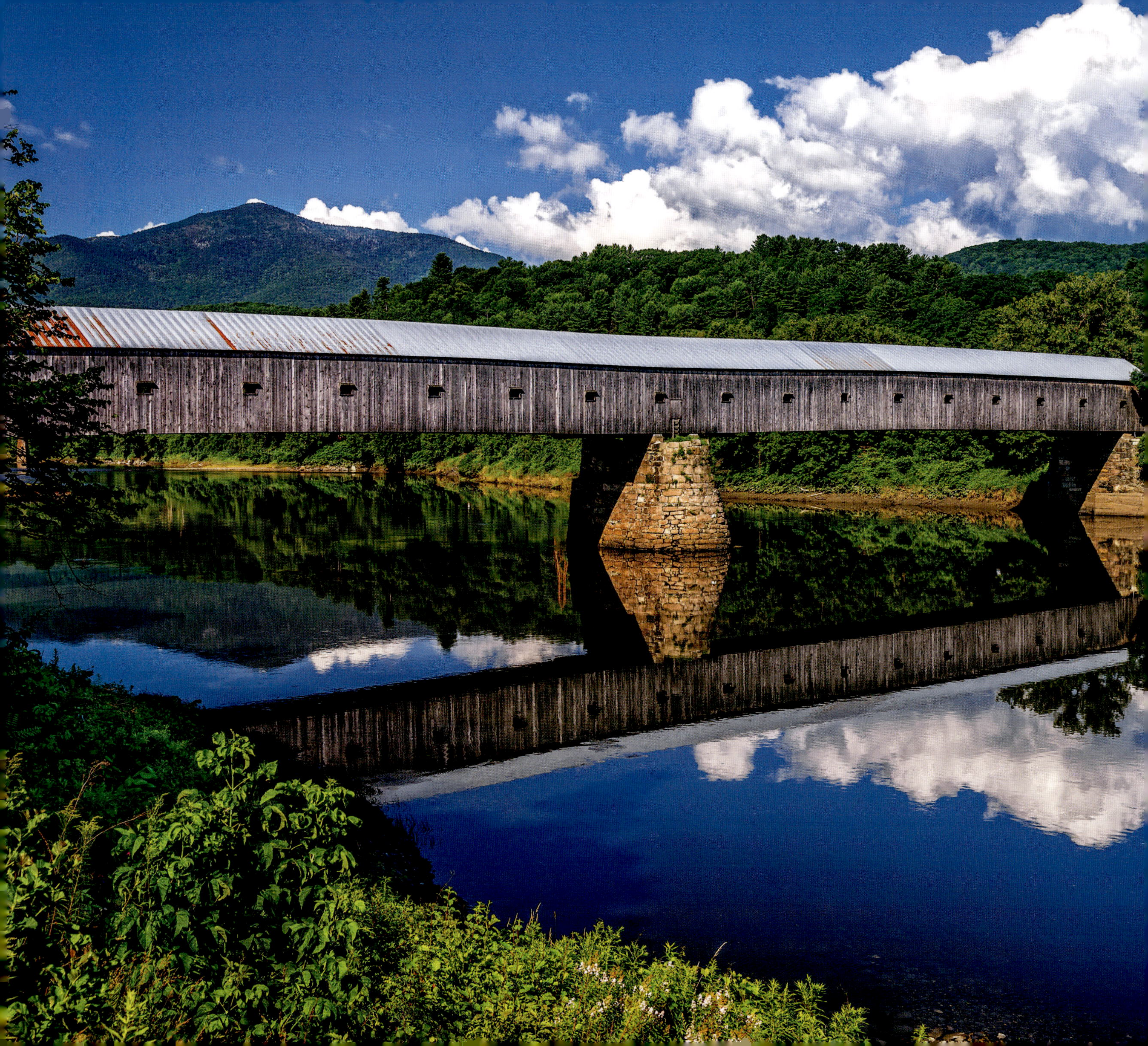

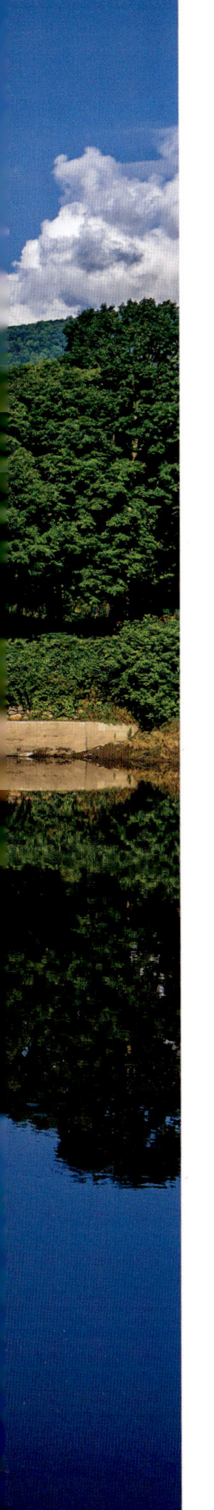

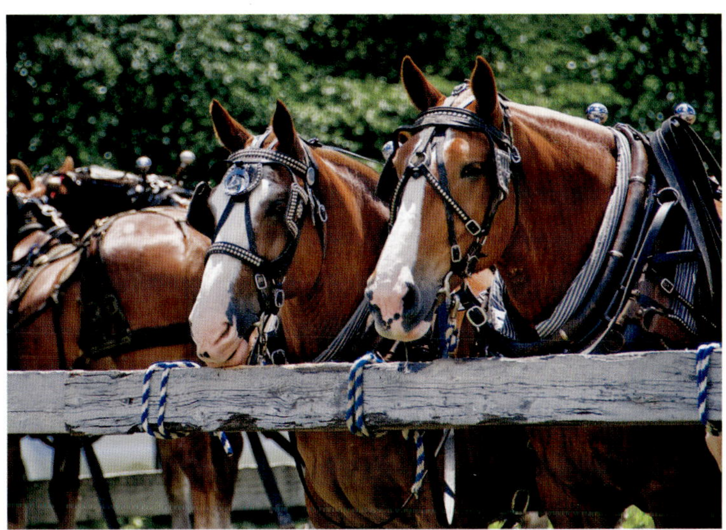

Left: Entrants wait patiently to show off their strength in the pulling contest at New Boston's Independence Day celebration, which has been called New Hampshire's "Best Patriotic Small Town Event." Their celebrity cousins, Budweiser Clydesdales, train in nearby Merrimack.

Far left: Car traffic still rumbles over the stunning 449-foot-long Cornish-Windsor Covered Bridge, the longest wooden covered bridge in the United States. Constructed in 1866, the double-span bridge extends across the Connecticut River to connect New Hampshire and Vermont.

Below: Calm waters of the beautiful Salmon Falls River flow through Somersworth, near the coastal border with Maine.

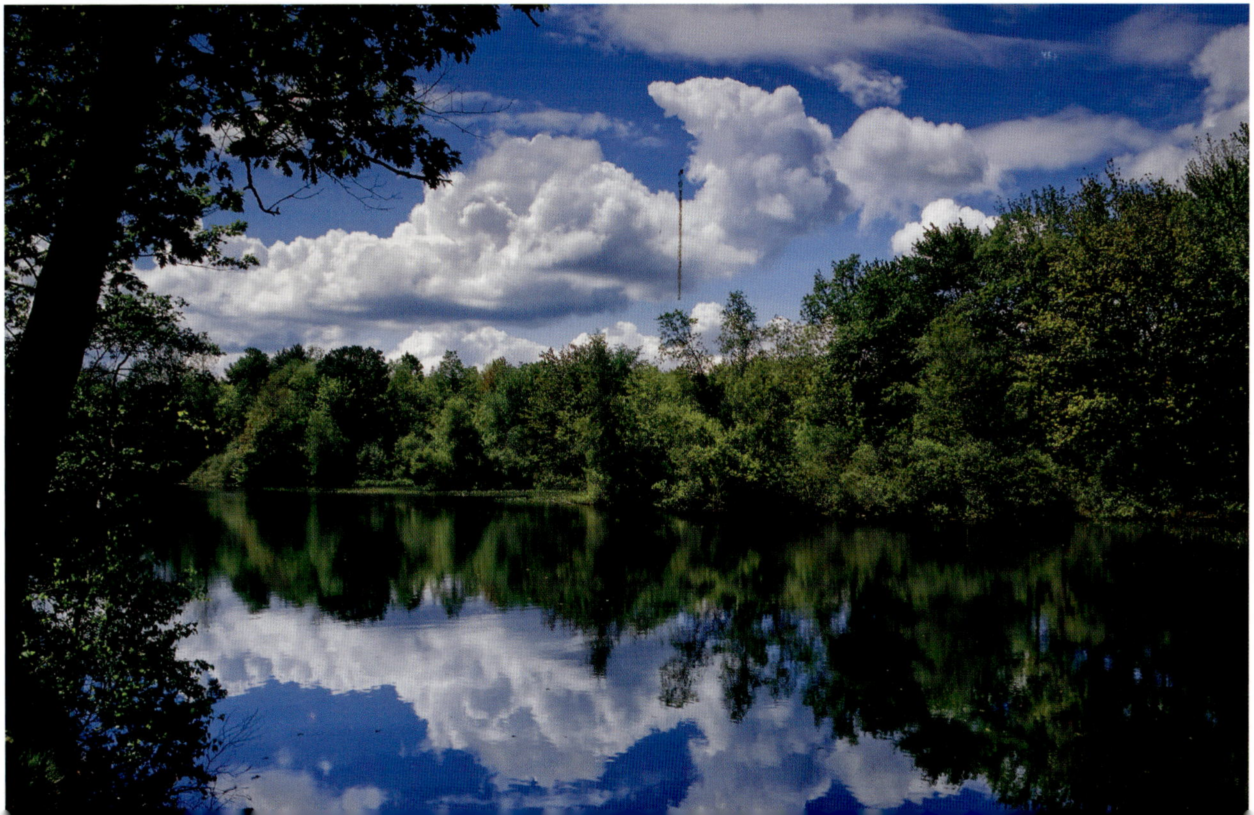

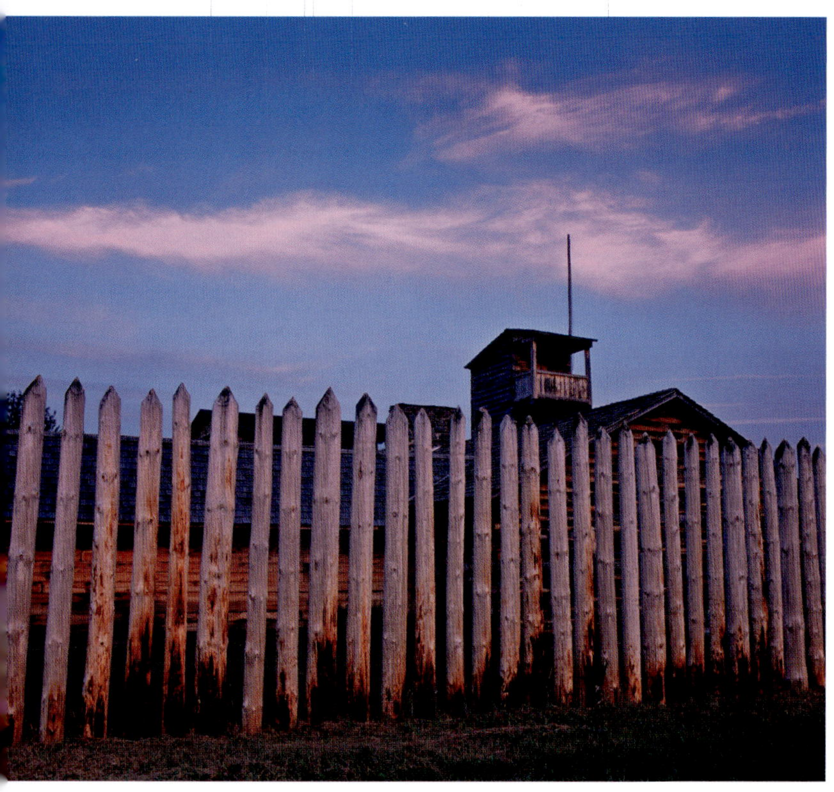

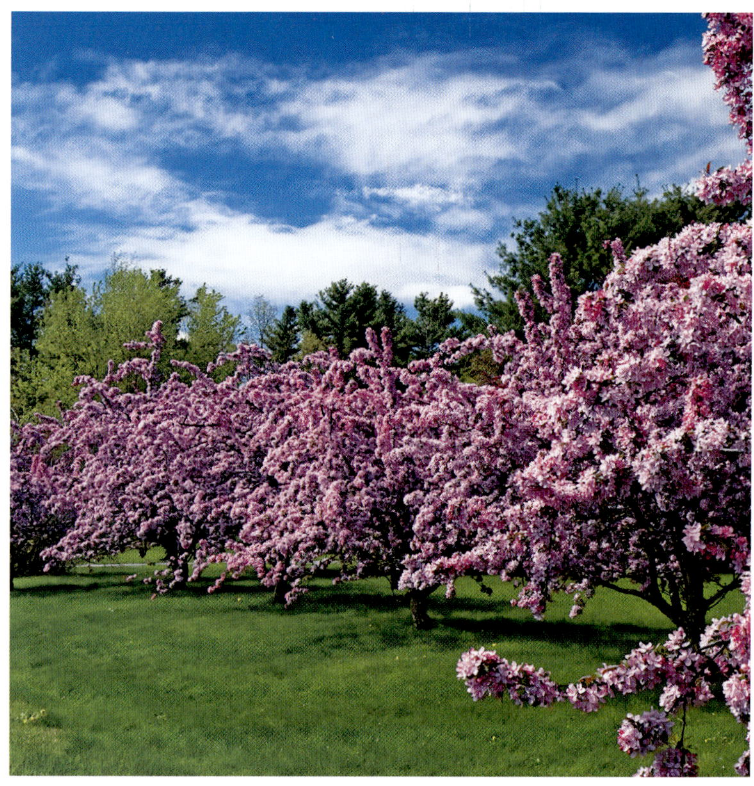

Above, left: The Fort at No. 4 in Charlestown, a living history museum, marks the site of the northernmost settlement of the English colonies in the 1740s. Erected near French trappers and the Abenaki tribe, the fort played an important role during the French and Indian War.

Above right: Spring blossoms at fruit orchards, like these flowering crabapples near Hollis, enliven landscapes throughout the Granite State.

Facing page: Early morning's dramatic light meets its match in the stark beauty of the Isles of Shoals, nine rocky, barren islands six miles off the New Hampshire coast. White Island's first lighthouse was built in 1820 at the highest point on the island. The replacement tower, erected in 1855, is now part of White Island State Historic Site.

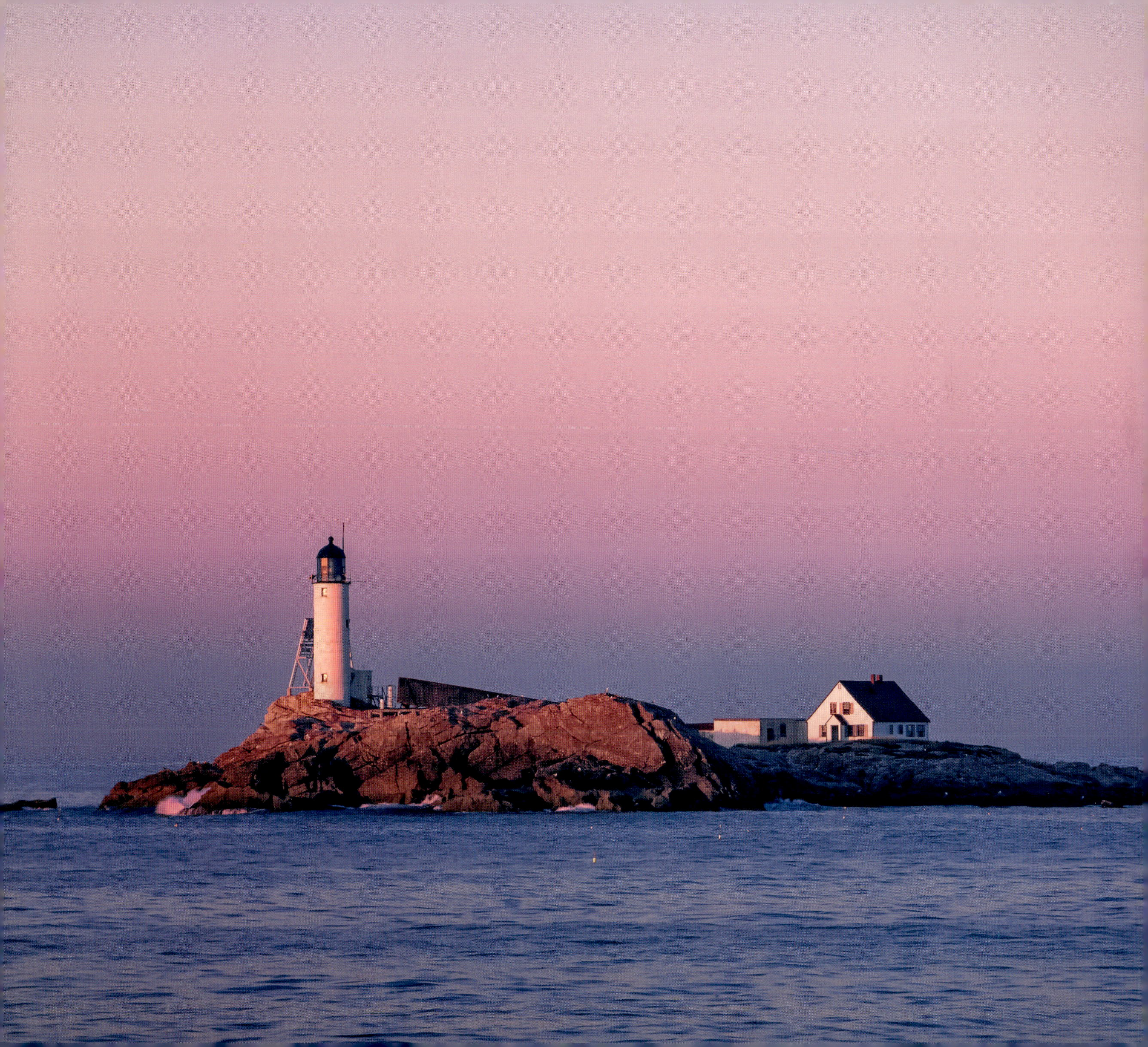

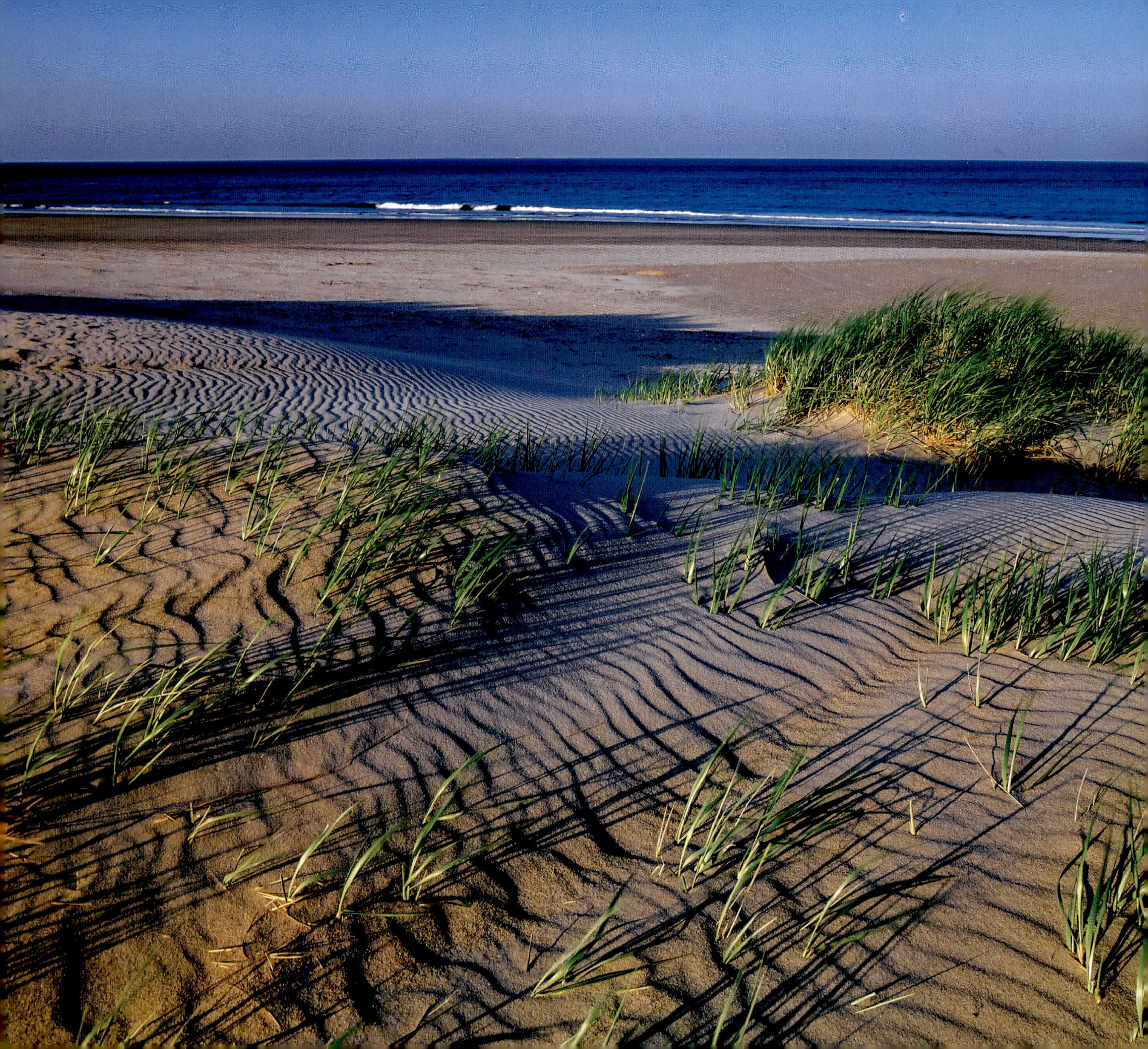

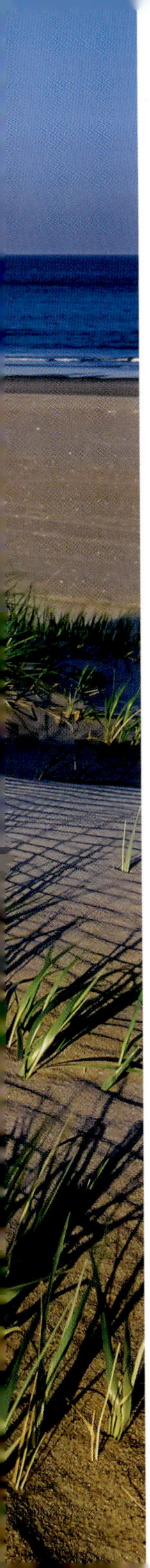

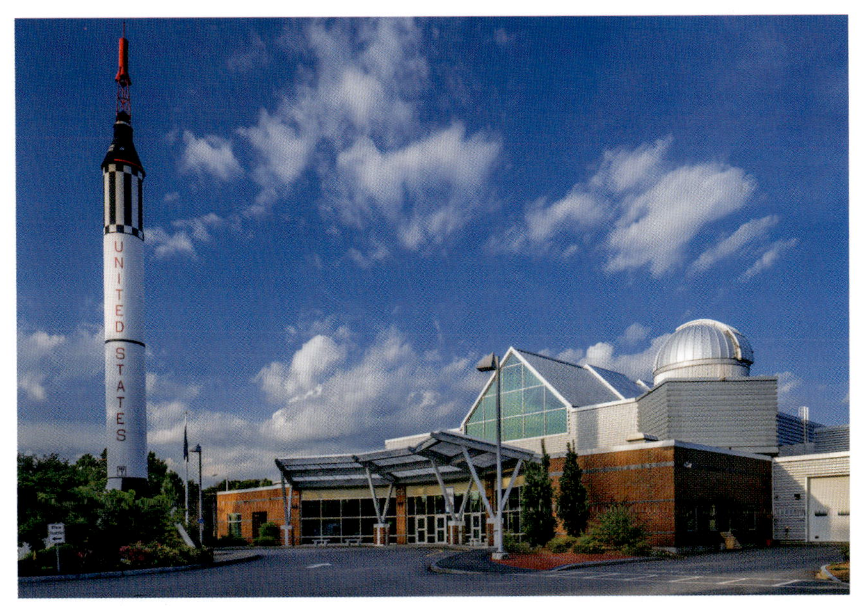

Left: A full-sized model of a Mercury-Redstone rocket outside the McAuliffe-Shepard Discovery Center in Concord ignites imagination and curiosity. The air and space science center honors the lives of Concord High School teacher and Teacher-in-Space Christa McAuliffe and Alan Shepard, the first American in space, born nearby in Derry.

Far left: Beach grass helps anchor sand dunes against the elements at Hampton Beach, part of New Hampshire's thirteen miles of coastline.

Below: This granite double arch bridge between Stoddard and Antrim was built in 1852 without mortar. It is one of several surviving examples of arched stone bridges in the Contoocook River Valley.

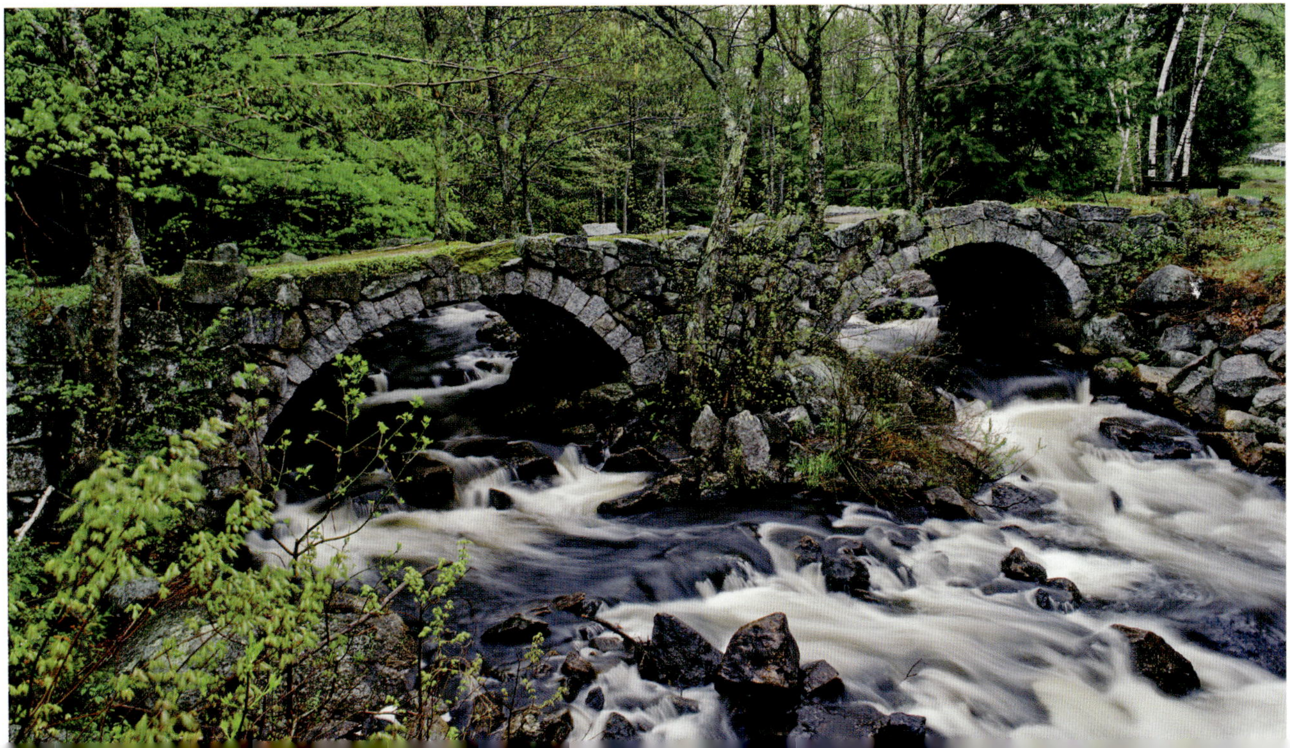

Right: Hardy adventurers hit the frigid water in Franklin and tackle the Winnipesaukee River's rapids on New Year's Day.

Far right: Christmas lights at dusk bring a pretty glow to Meredith, a restored mill village on the shores of Lake Winnipesaukee. At seventy-two square miles, the lake is the largest in the state and the showpiece of the Lakes Region.

Below: Once called "courting bridges," covered bridges in the White Mountains provide shelter from unexpected storms. Albany Bridge, near the town of Albany, has offered safe crossing over the Swift River since 1858.

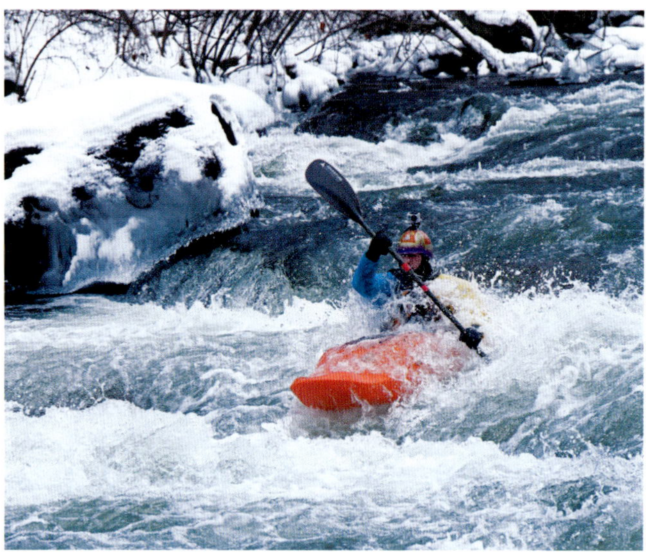

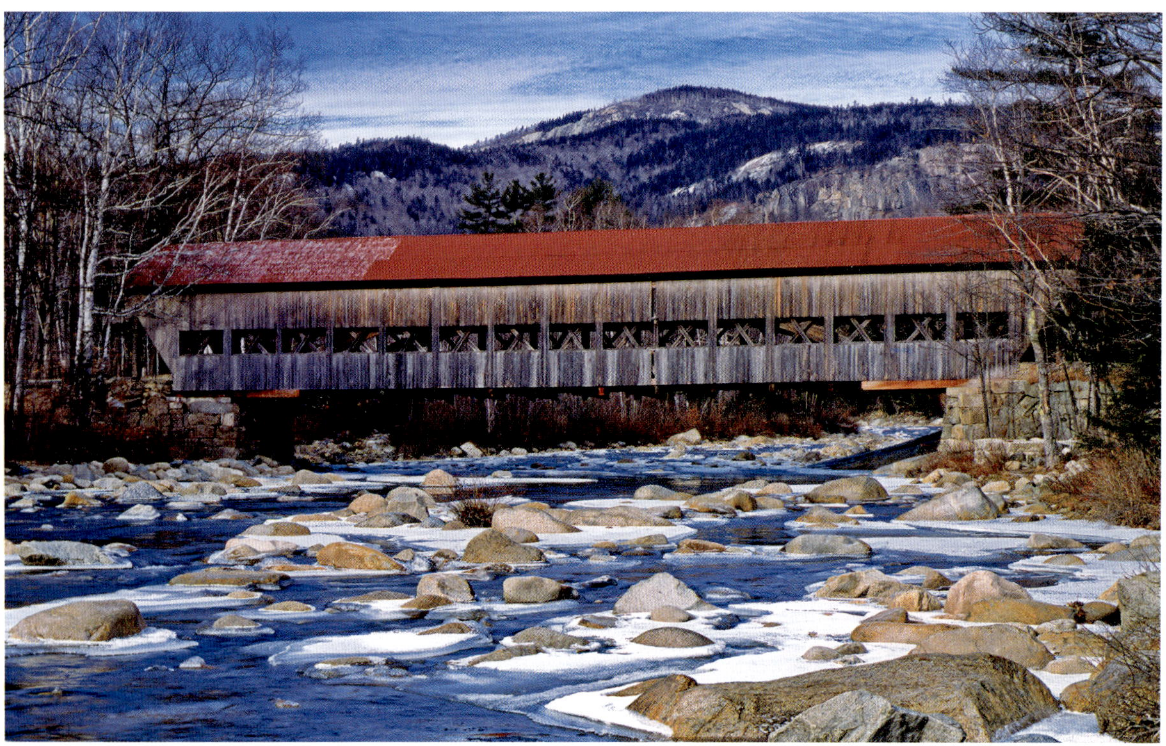

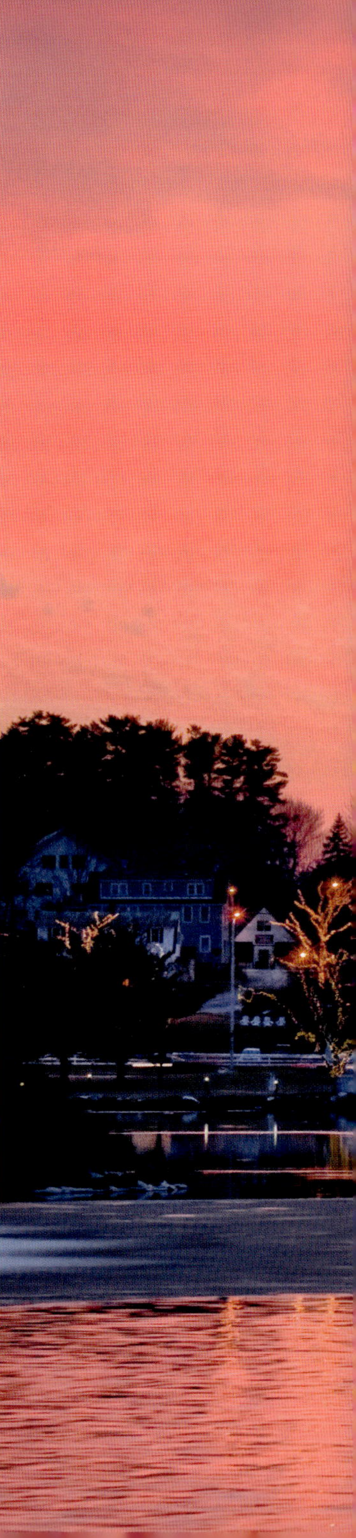

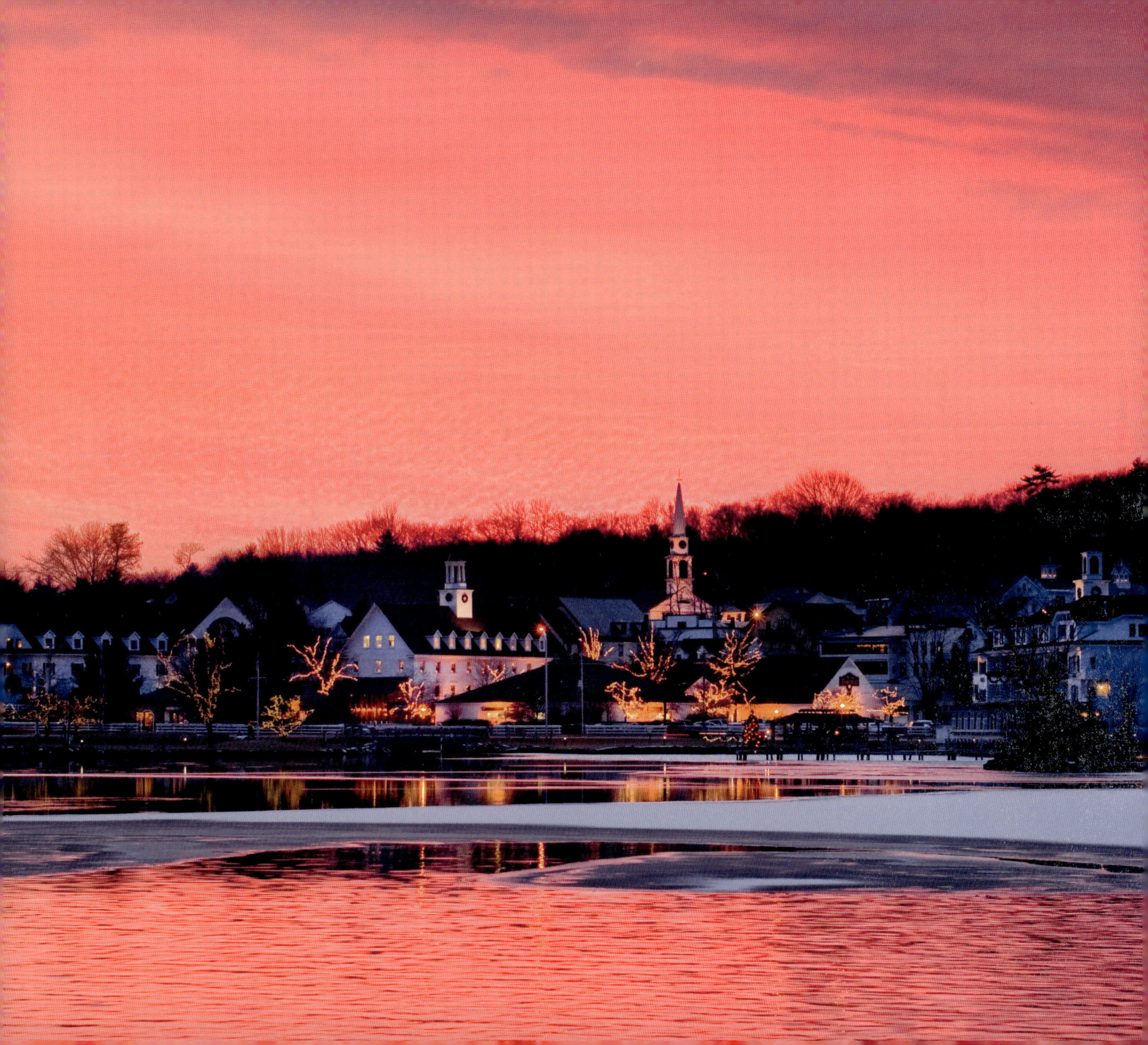

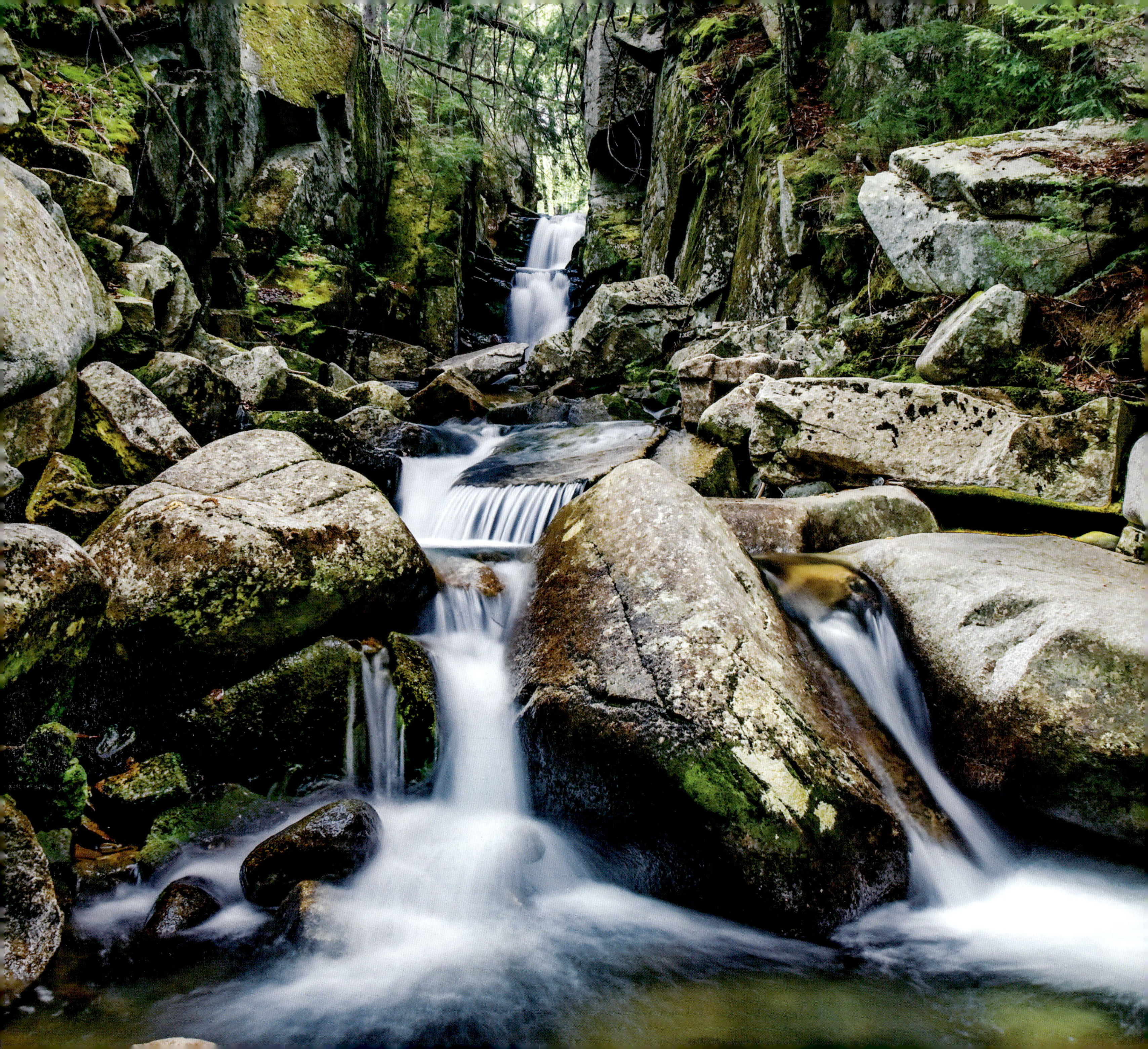

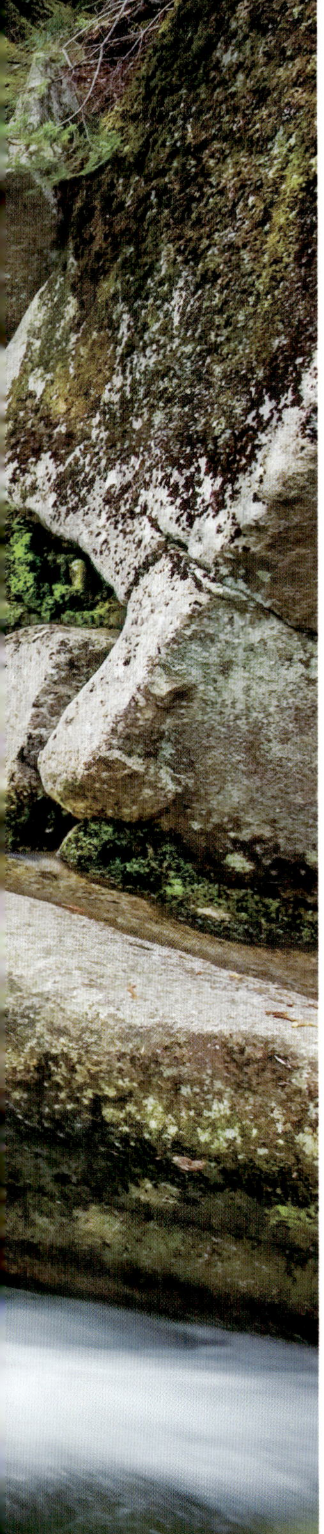

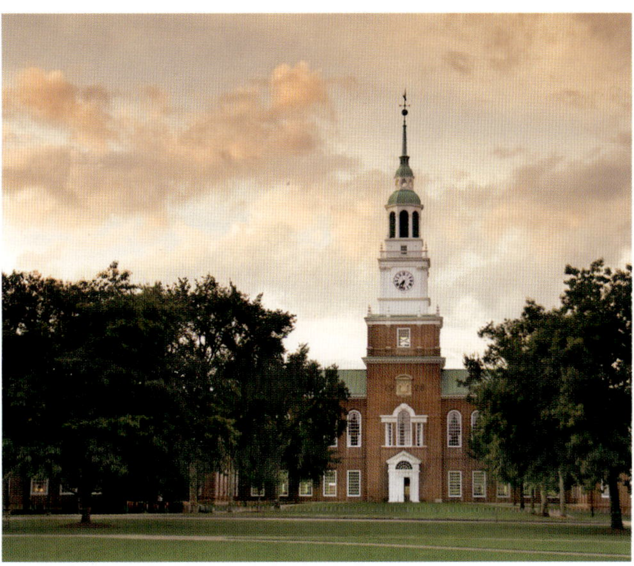

Left: The Baker-Berry Library is the proud symbol of Dartmouth College. Founded in 1769, Dartmouth is a prestigious Ivy League institution.

Far left: Flume Brook skids over the boulders to form Baby Flume in the Great North Woods' Dixville Notch State Park.

Below: Gap Mountain, near Troy, is known for its abundance of wild blueberries and spectacular views of the 3,165-foot granite peak of Mount Monadnock, which is among the most-climbed mountains in the world.

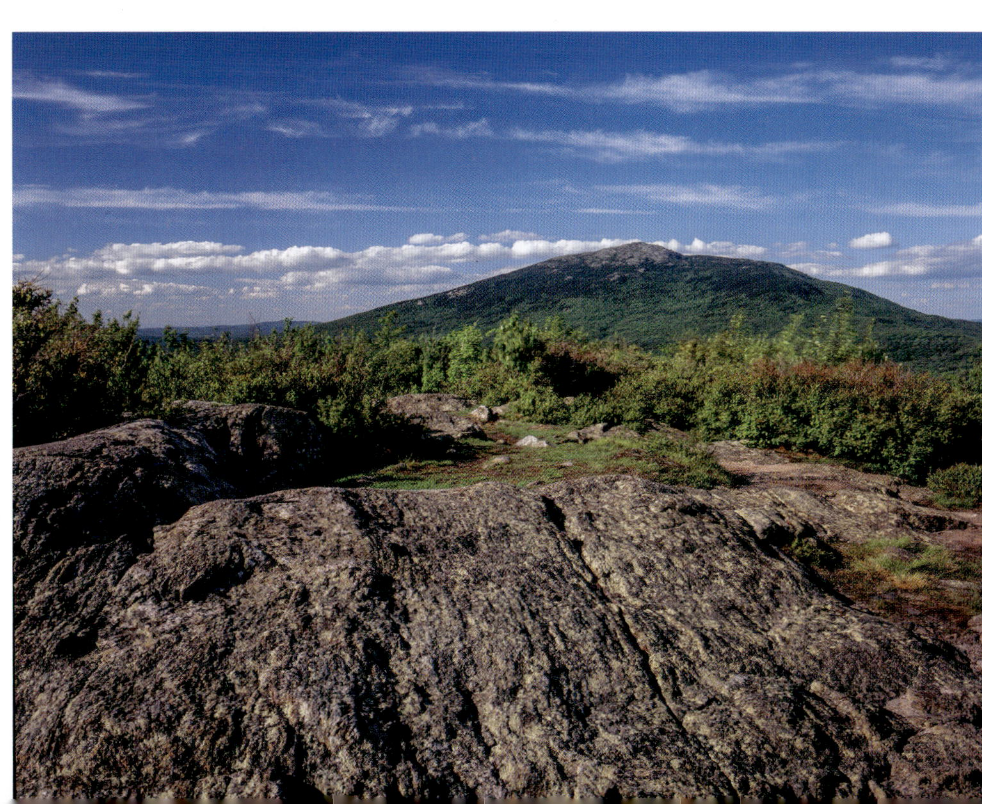

Right: Jeffers Brook tumbles through Benton, surrounded by the beauty of the White Mountains.

Far right: An old red mill on a misty morning is a reminder that the Squam River powered some of Ashland's first mills, including a sawmill and a gristmill.

Below: Hoping for trout, anglers cast their lines into the deep waters of Dublin Lake. The picturesque lake hosted summer resident Mark Twain in 1905 and 1906.

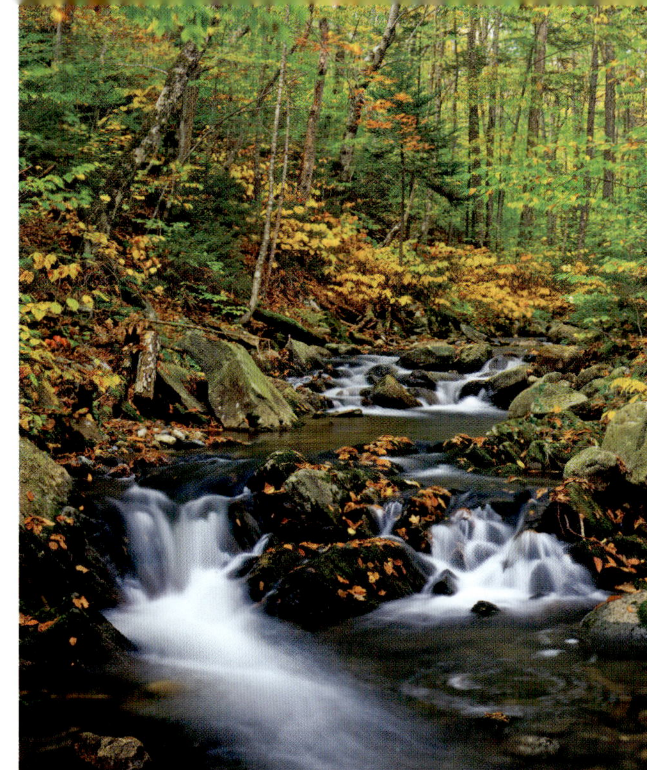

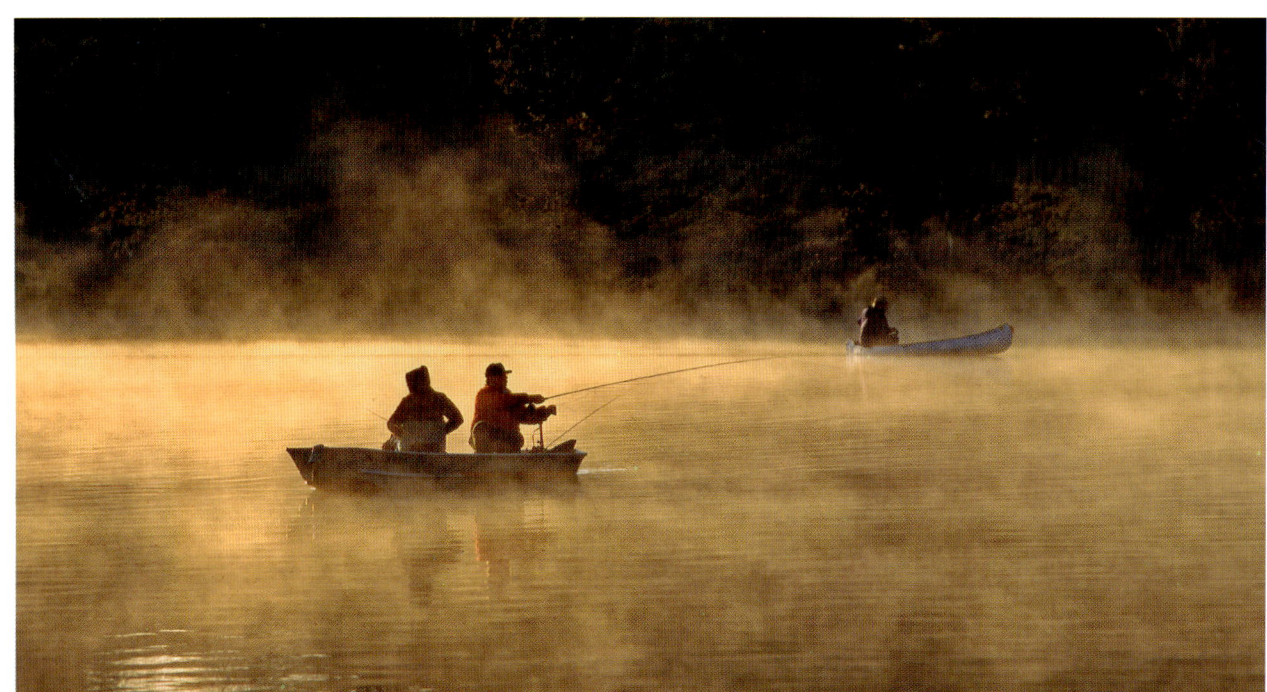

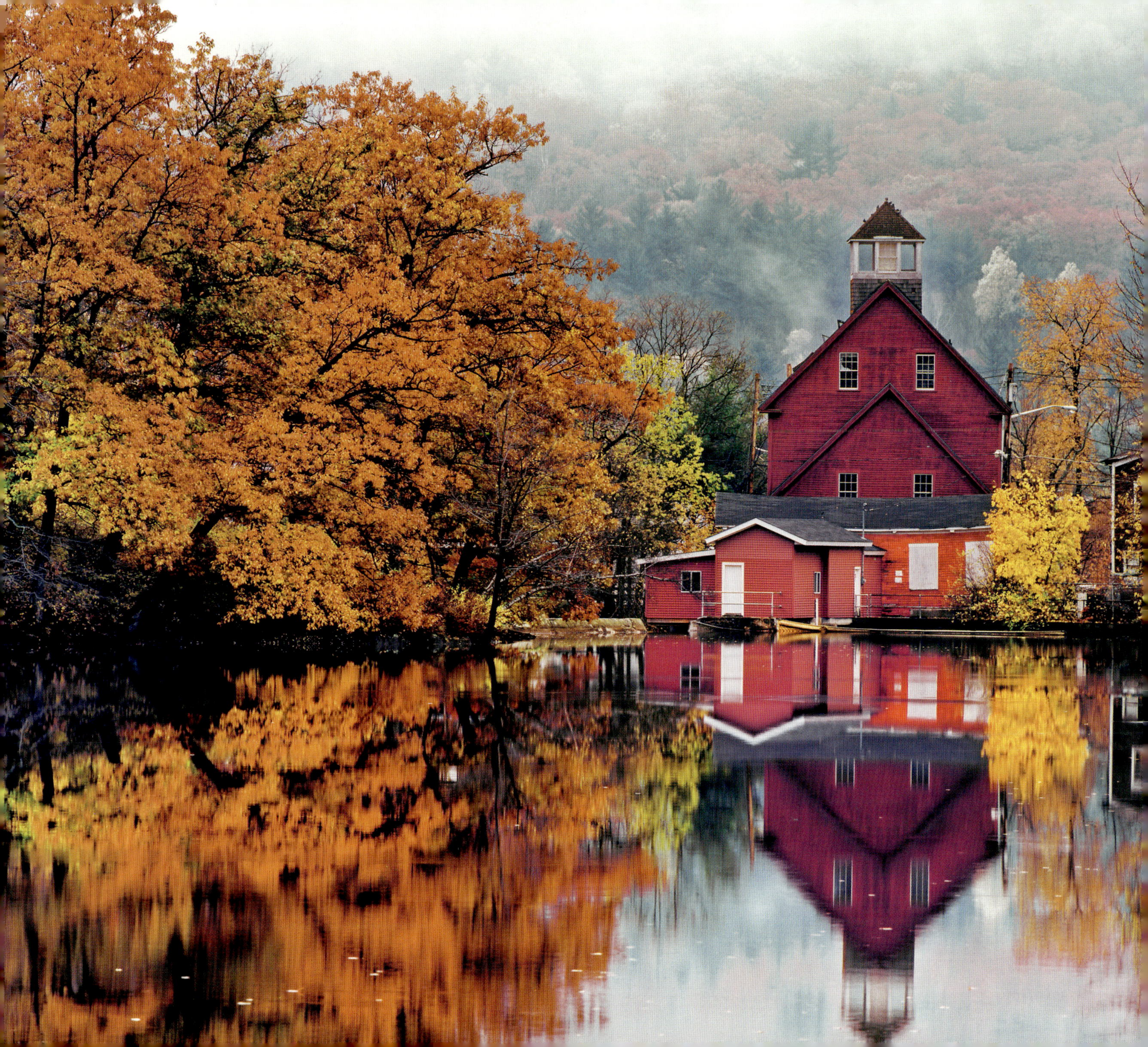

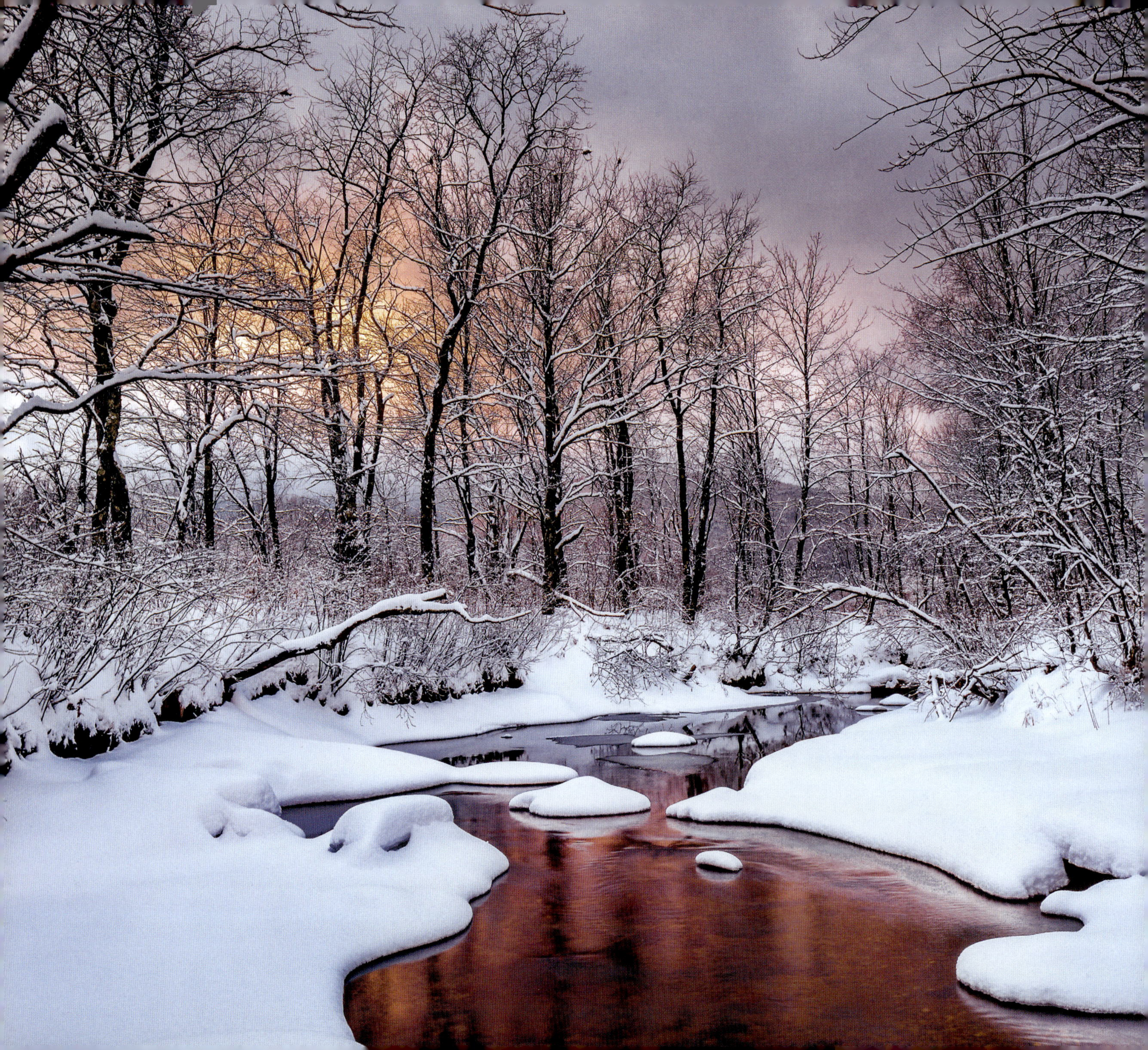

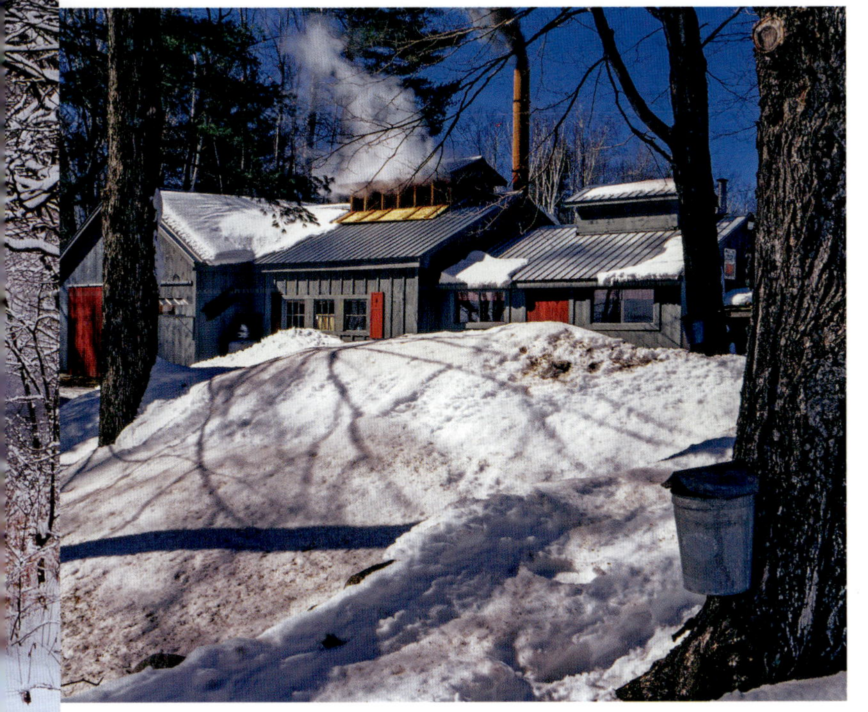

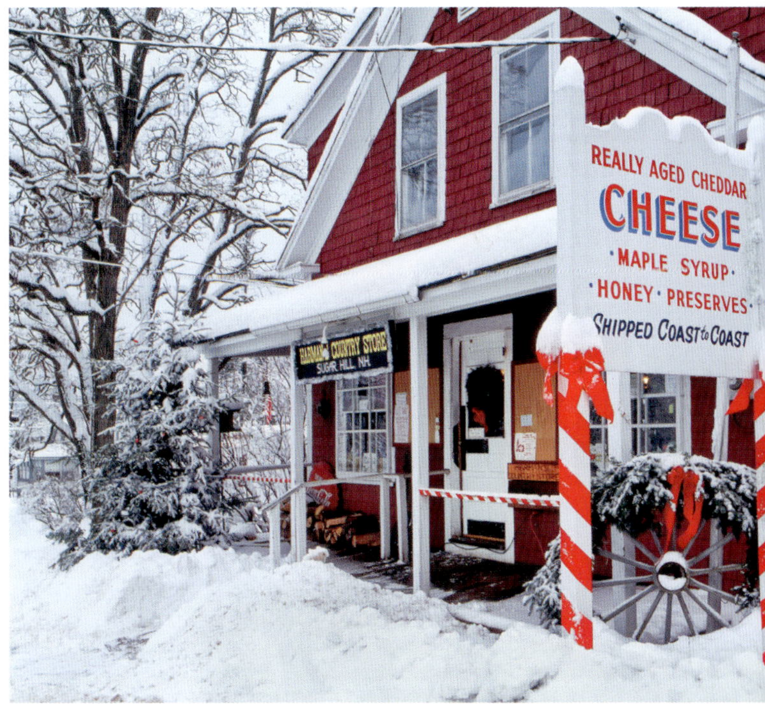

Above left: Clouds of steam billow from the Maple Tree Farm sugarhouse in the town of Hill. Roughly forty gallons of sap are boiled down to make a single gallon of sublimely sticky maple syrup.

Above right: Since 1955, country staples like local honey, aged cheddar, and maple syrup have drawn customers to Harman's Cheese & Country Store in Sugar Hill. Country stores are a beloved New Hampshire tradition, sharing their hometown flavors with locals and New England enthusiasts nationwide.

Far left: Silence and solitude settle over the Whiteface River as the sun goes down in the Lakes Region near the town of Sandwich.

Right: Winter moves through the Granite State, sweeping down from the north and sometimes meeting up with autumn where snow and foliage paint the mountainside.

Far right: Basking in sunlight, the Waterloo Covered Bridge was constructed to span the Warner River in 1840.

Below: The state's second-largest city, Nashua frequently makes national lists of Best Places to Live. Its striking, Romanesque-style First Congregational Church was built in 1893 of New Hampshire granite.

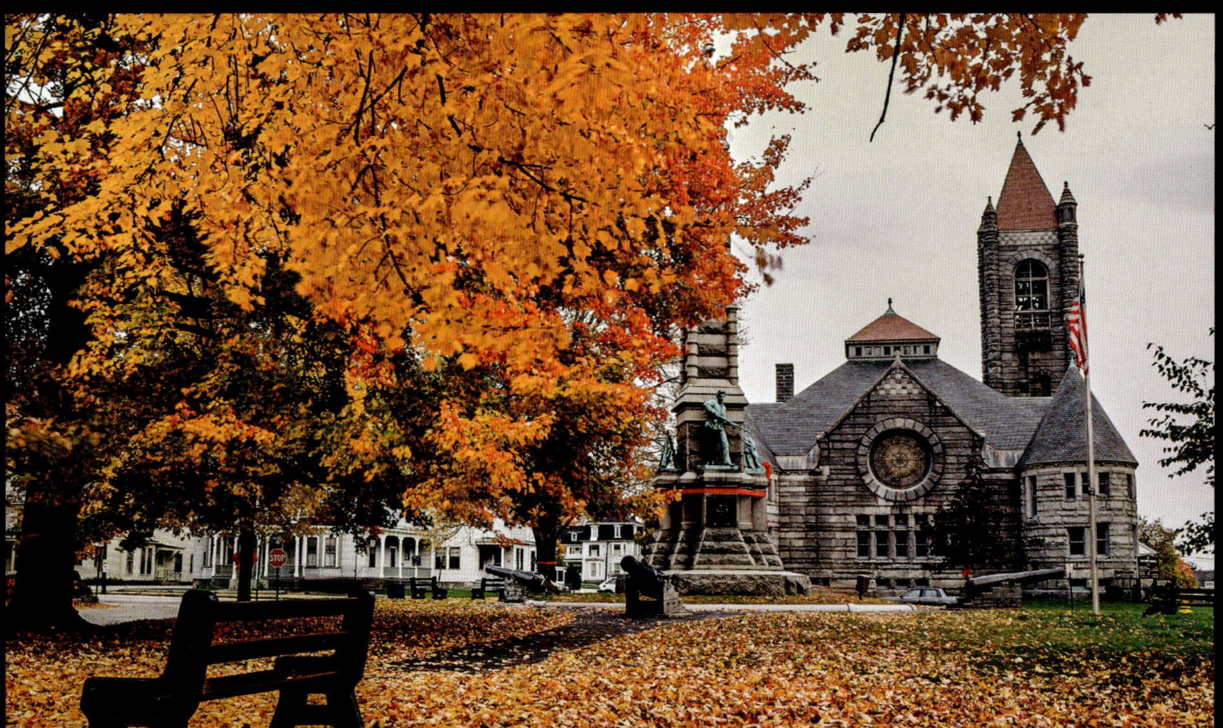

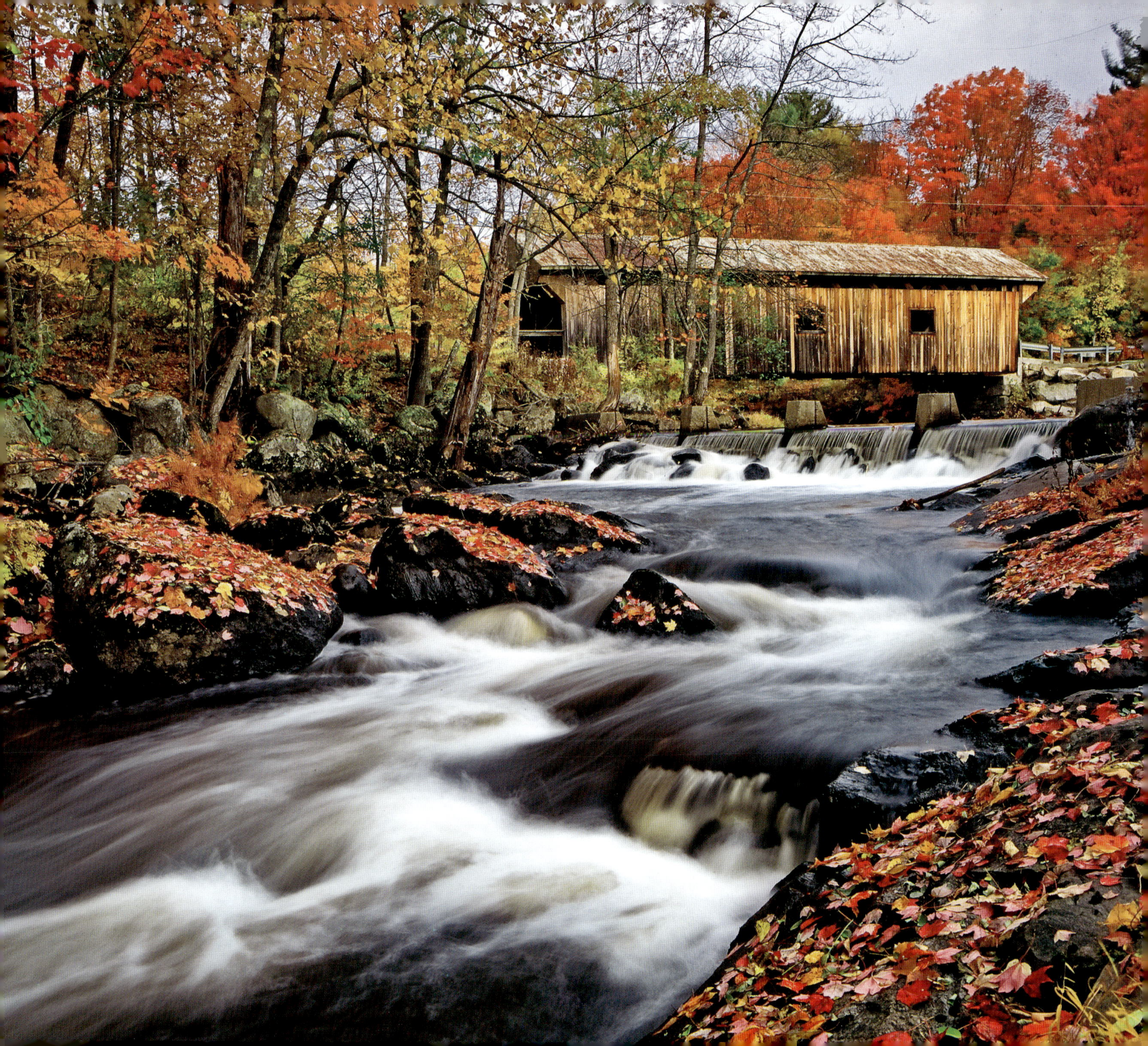

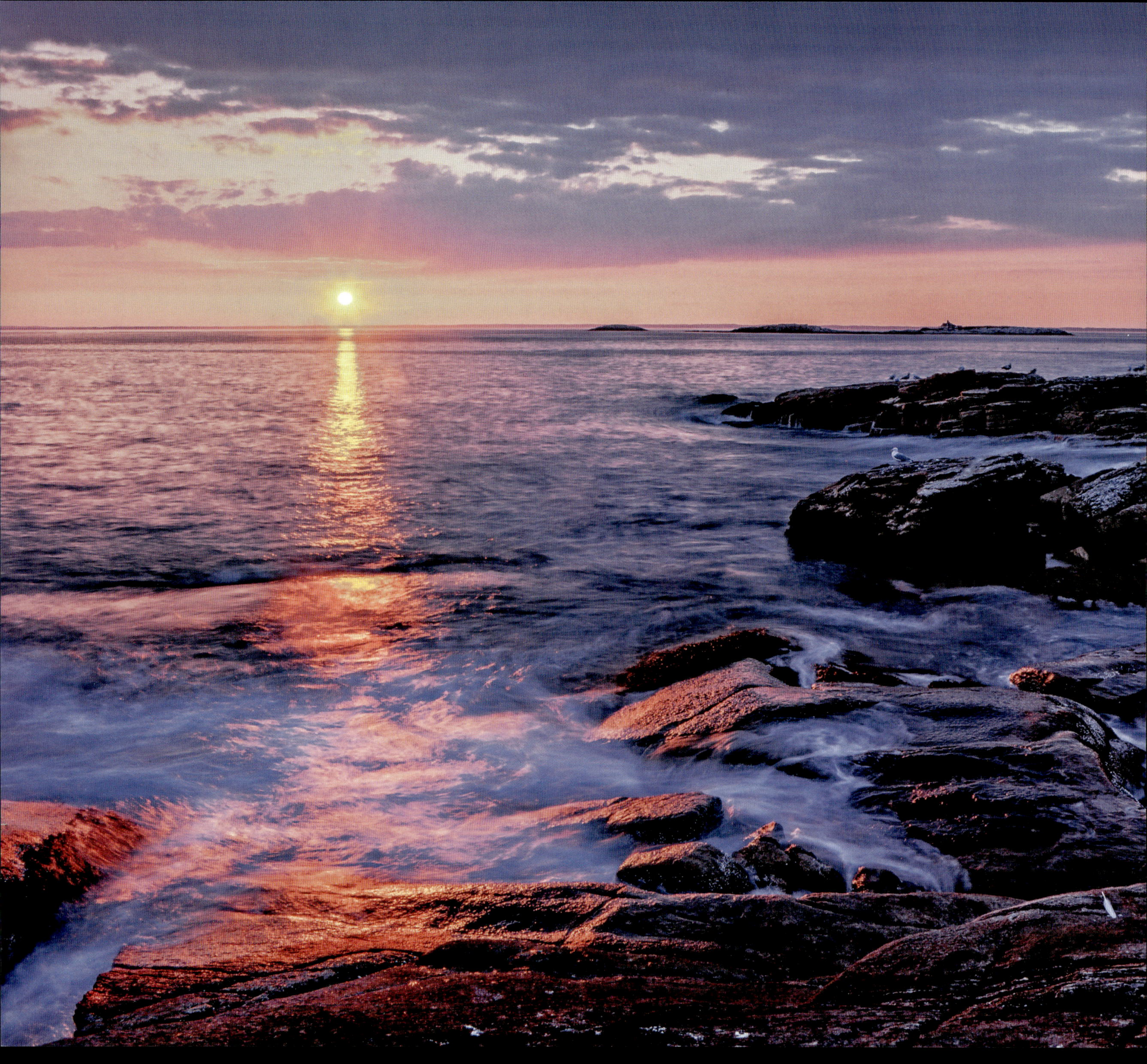

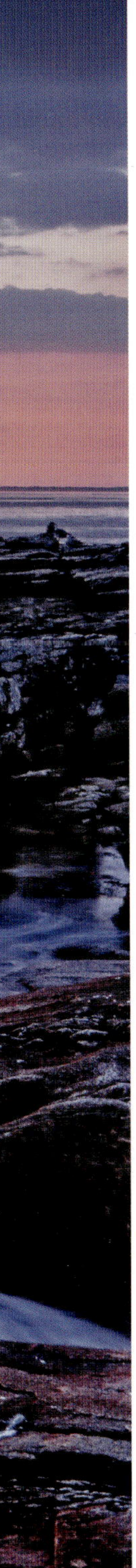

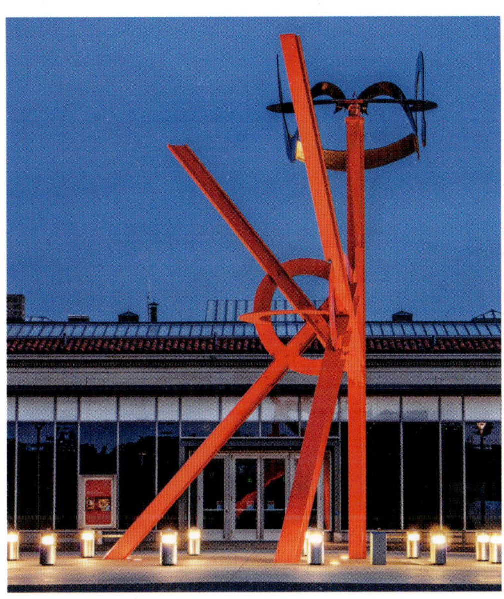

Left: The kinetic sculpture *Origins* by Mark di Suvero greets visitors to Manchester's Currier Museum of Art, an elegant collection that includes works by Monet, Picasso, and O'Keeffe, plus the Zimmerman House, its very own Frank Lloyd Wright house.

Mark di Suvero, American, b. 1933, *Origins*, 2001-2004, steel and painted, Currier Museum of Art, Manchester, New Hampshire. Museum Purchase: The Henry Melville Fuller Acquisition Fund, 2006.51

Far left: Sunset imitates a lighthouse, casting reflections over the rocky shore surrounding Star Island in the Isles of Shoals off the coast of Portsmouth.

Below: Warm holiday lights glow, pretty as a snow globe, as night gathers in Stark. Popular with artists, its 1862 covered bridge washed away in a flood in 1890, and the townspeople brought it back and placed it on new piers.

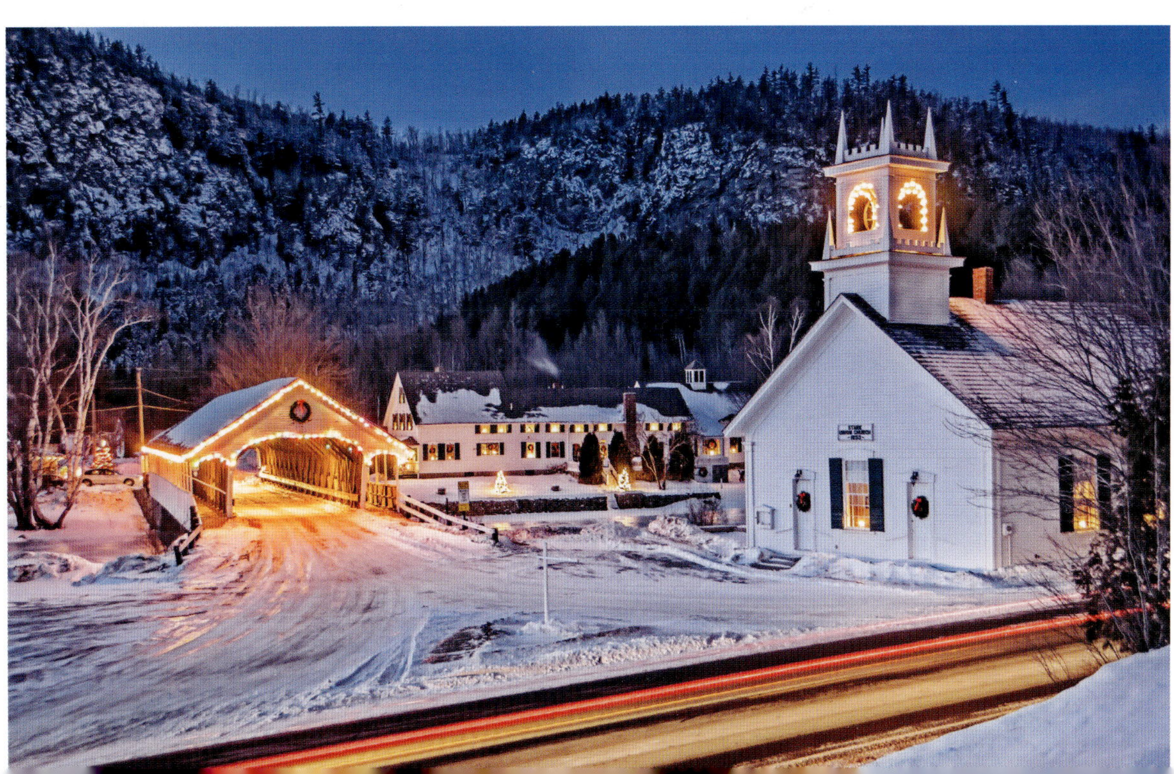

Right: Sabbaday Falls pours over the rocks near Waterville Valley, a resort town surrounded by White Mountain National Forest.

Far right: In 1808, the small, centrally located city of Concord was named the state capital. At the state house, a proud eagle glints against the sky and a statue of abolitionist Senator John P. Hale welcomes visitors to the 1816 gold-domed building.

Below: It's hard to imagine a more serene place than the placid Great North Woods setting of the Androscoggin River, edged with spring greenery and fir trees.

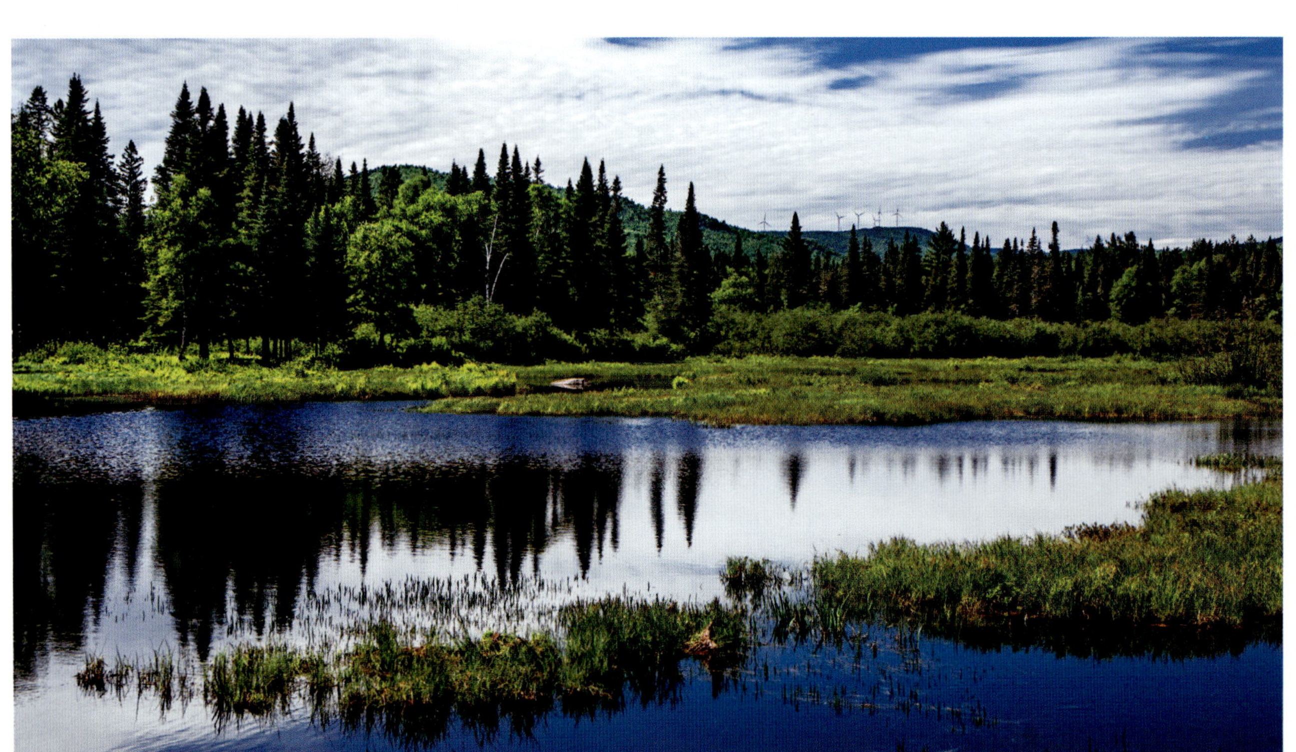

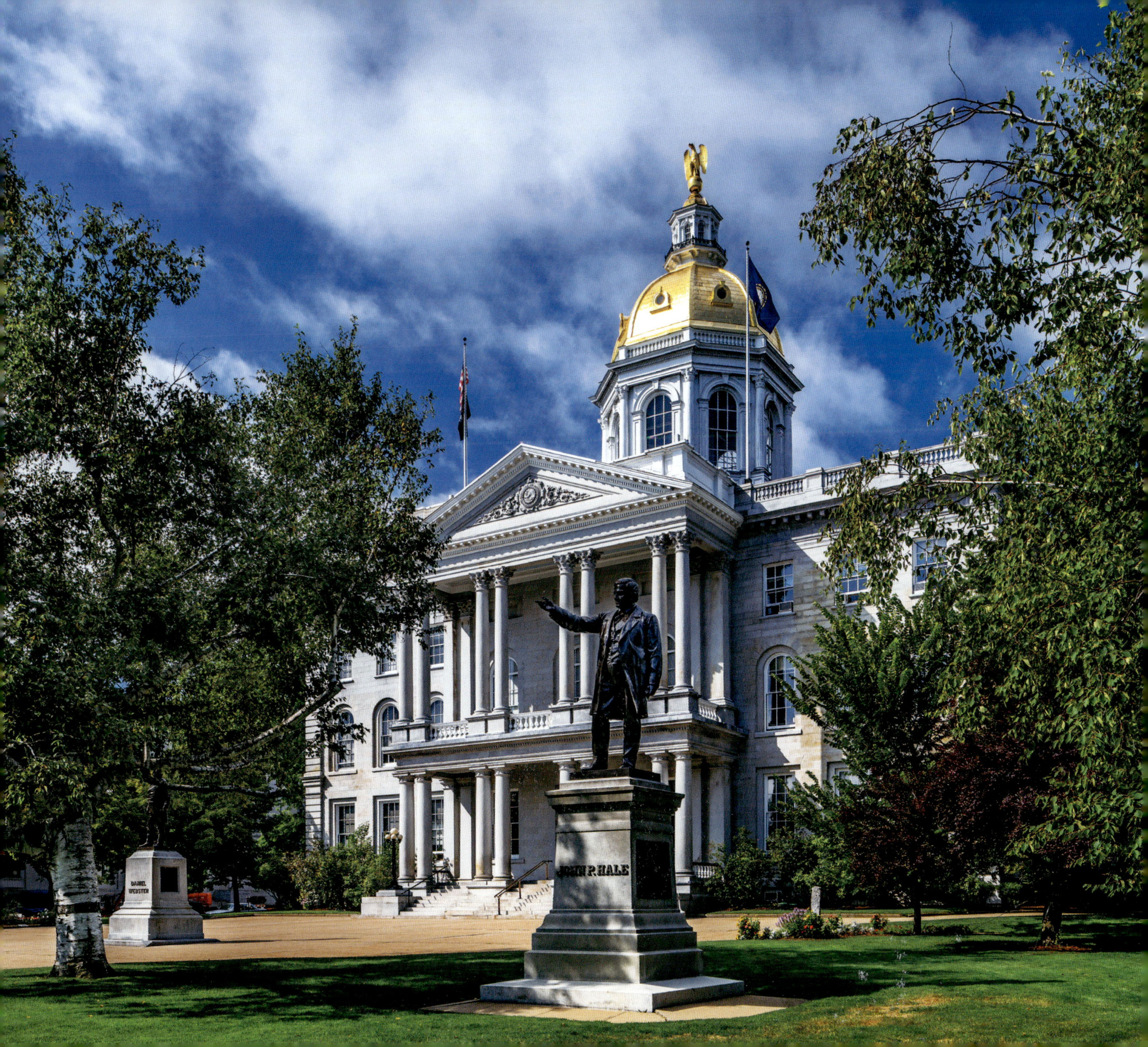
DANIEL
WEBSTER
JOHN P. HALE

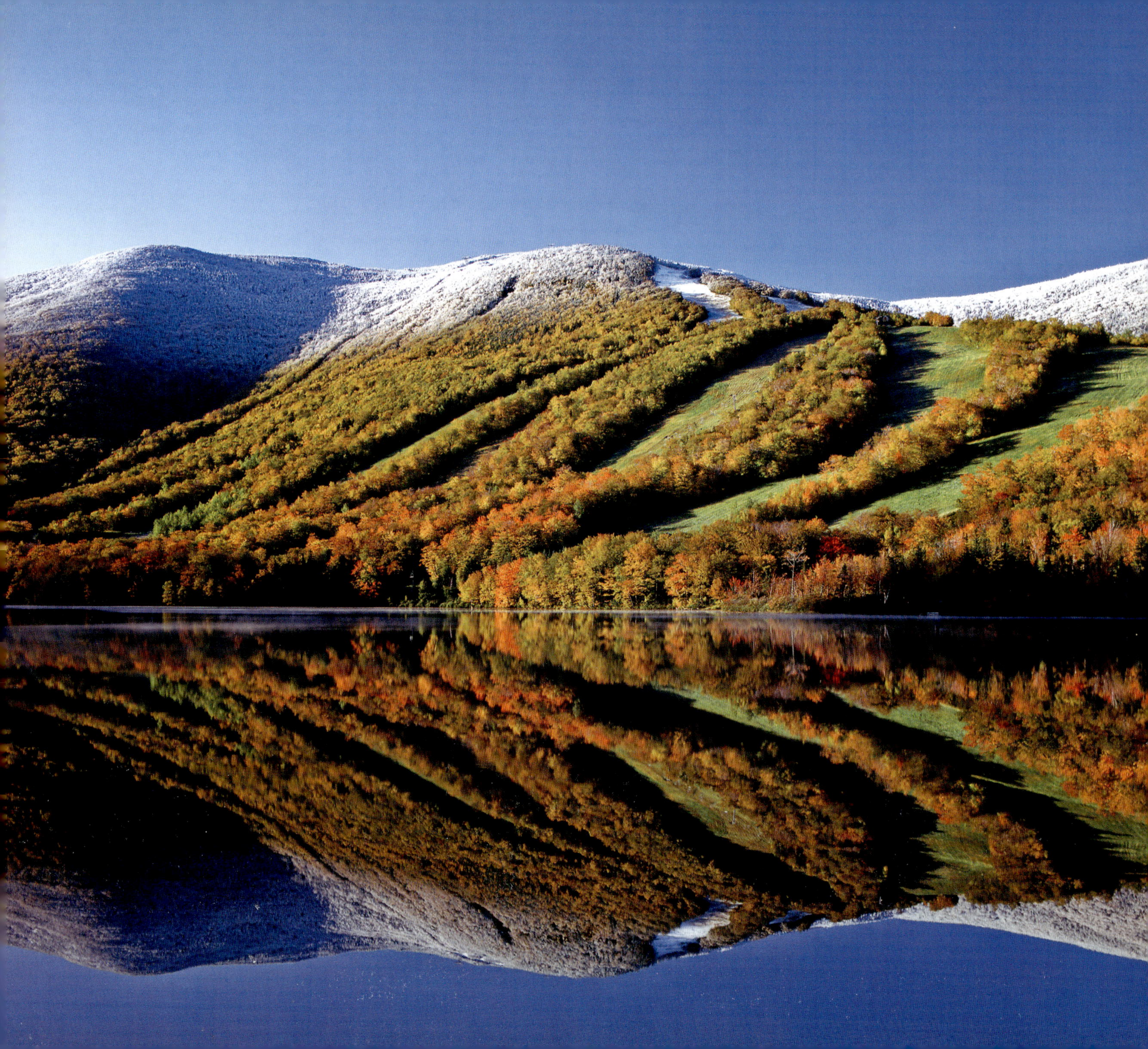

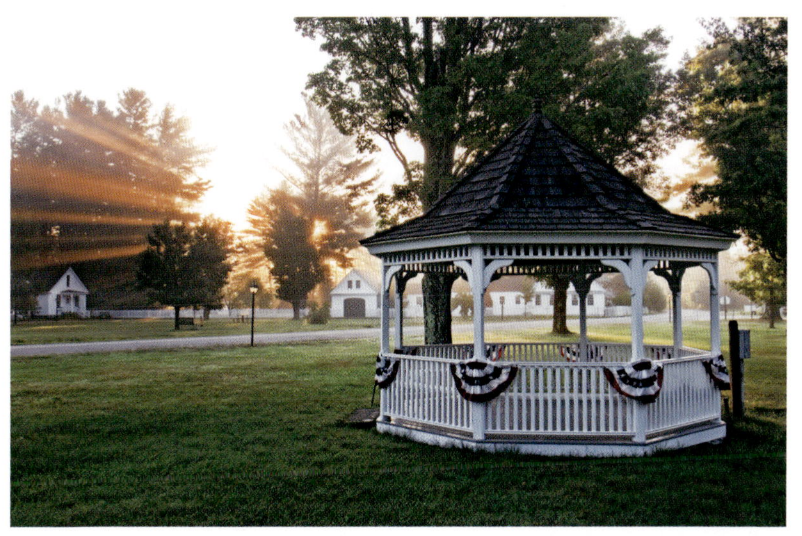

Left: Sunrise filters through the leaves on Hebron's town common and gazebo.

Far left: Ski trails escape a dusting at Cannon Mountain, beloved by local skiers. In autumn, an eighty-passenger tram takes "leaf peepers" to the top for views from the 4,080-foot summit. On a clear day, you can see Canada!

Below: A picture-perfect horse stable at Castle in the Clouds at Moultonborough looks toward autumn leaves.

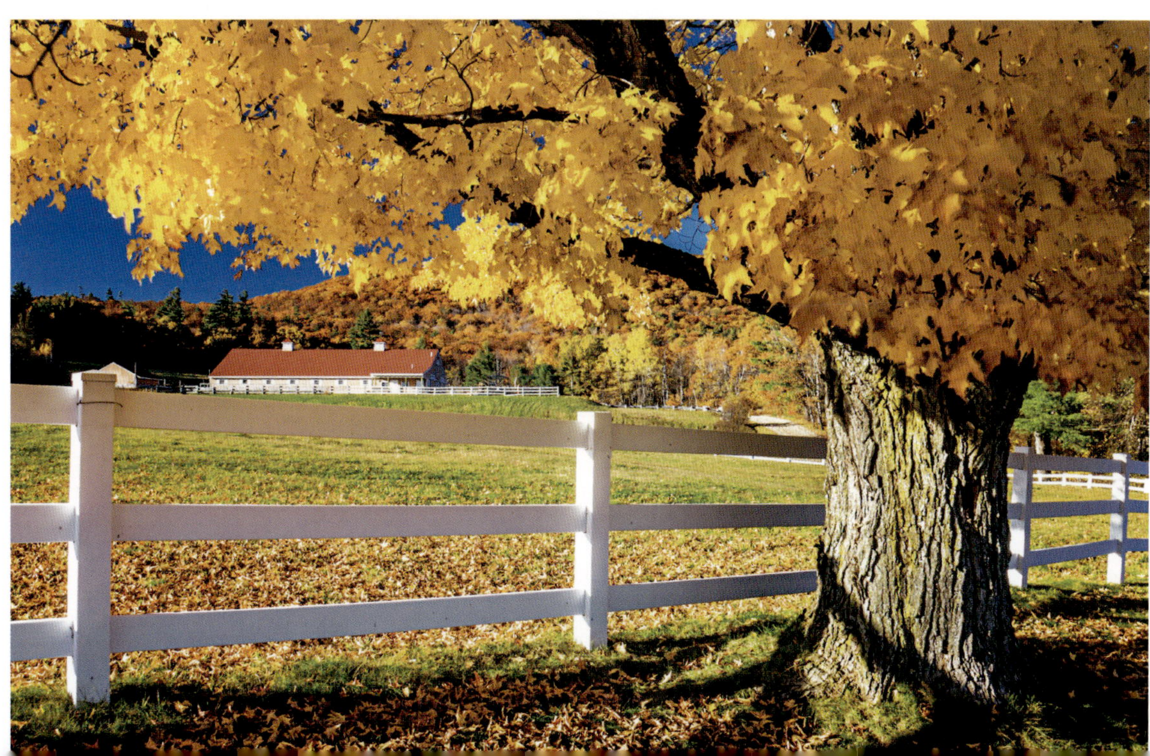

Right: The lovely white-tailed deer, strolling on Long Island, the largest island in Lake Winnipesaukee, was named the official state animal in 1983.

Far right: Rivulets pour down Beaver Brook Falls at the edge of Colebrook. The waterfall, easily accessible by all and just off Route 145, sweeps nearly 100 feet to the pool below.

Below: Marlow Town Hall, a church, and the Odd Fellows Hall join graceful white birches reflecting off Marlow Pond in the spring.

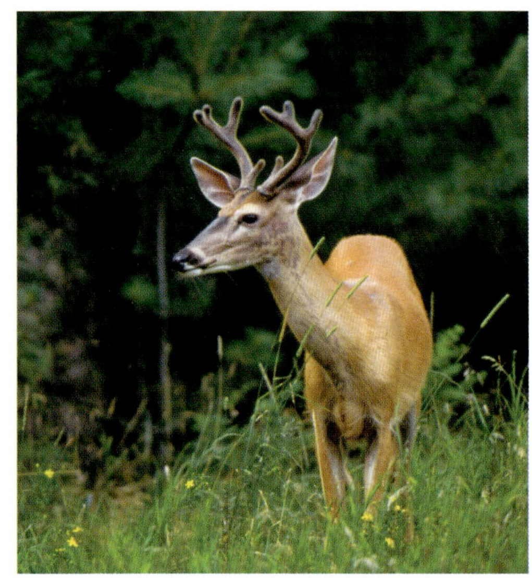

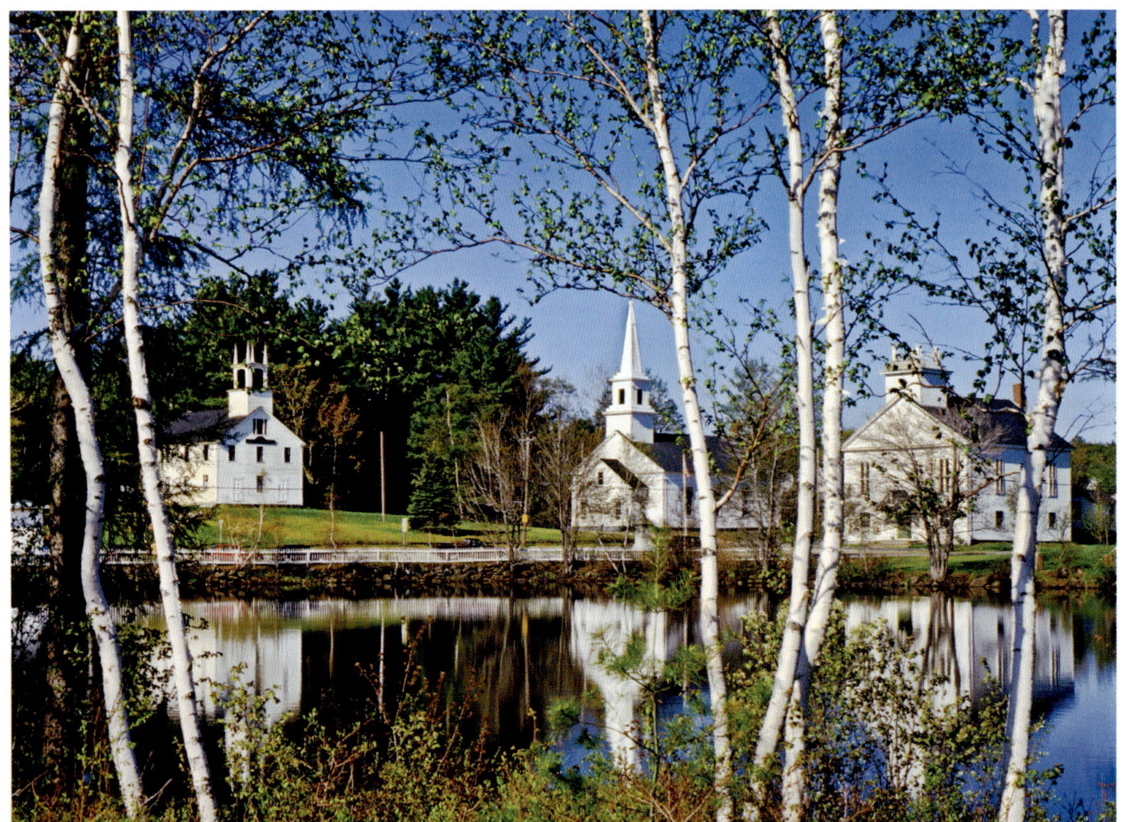

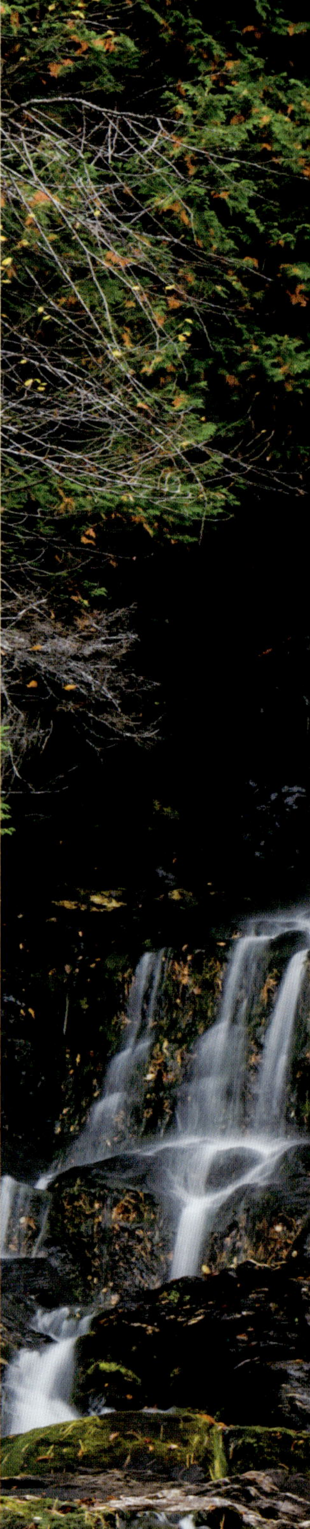

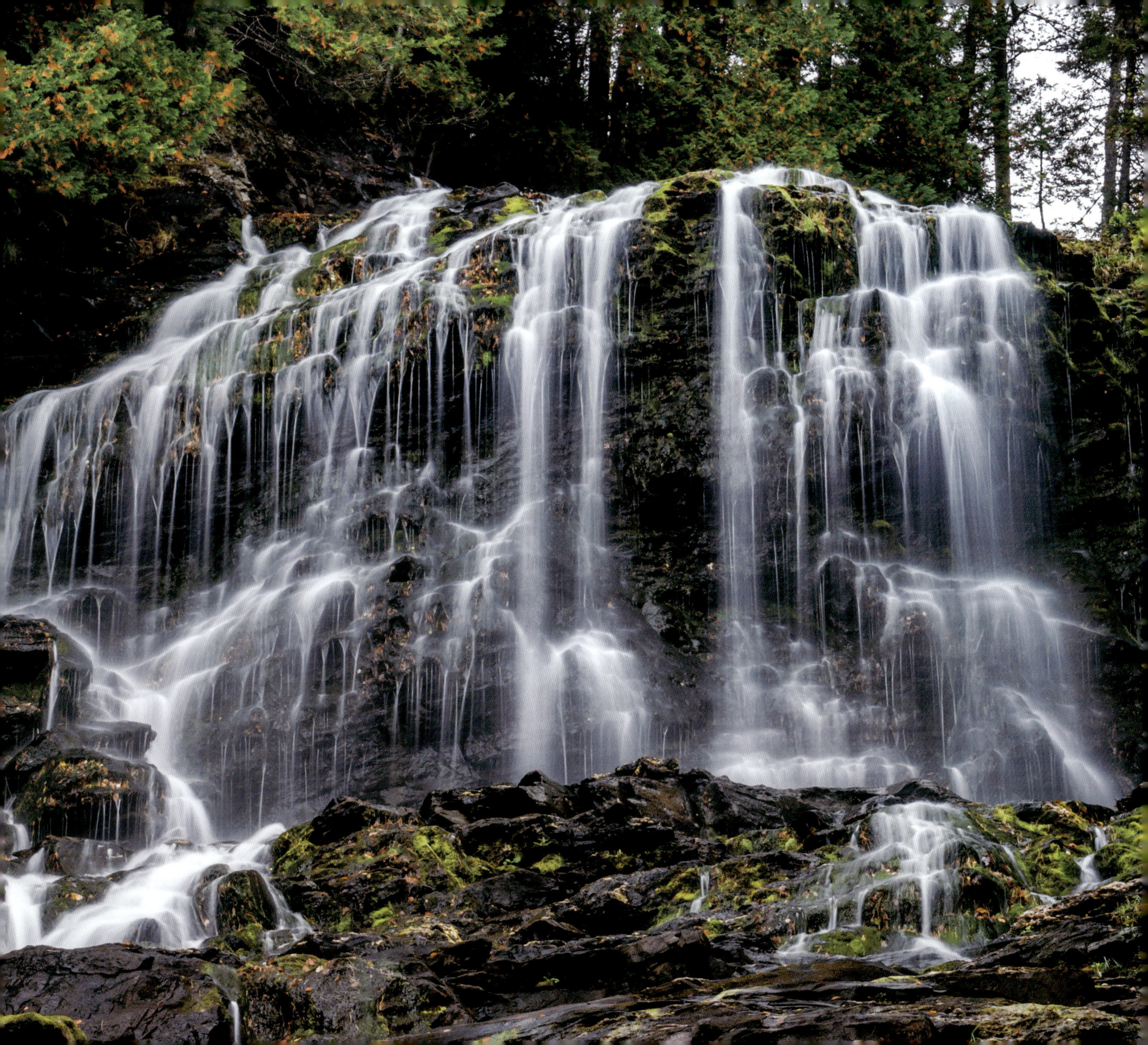

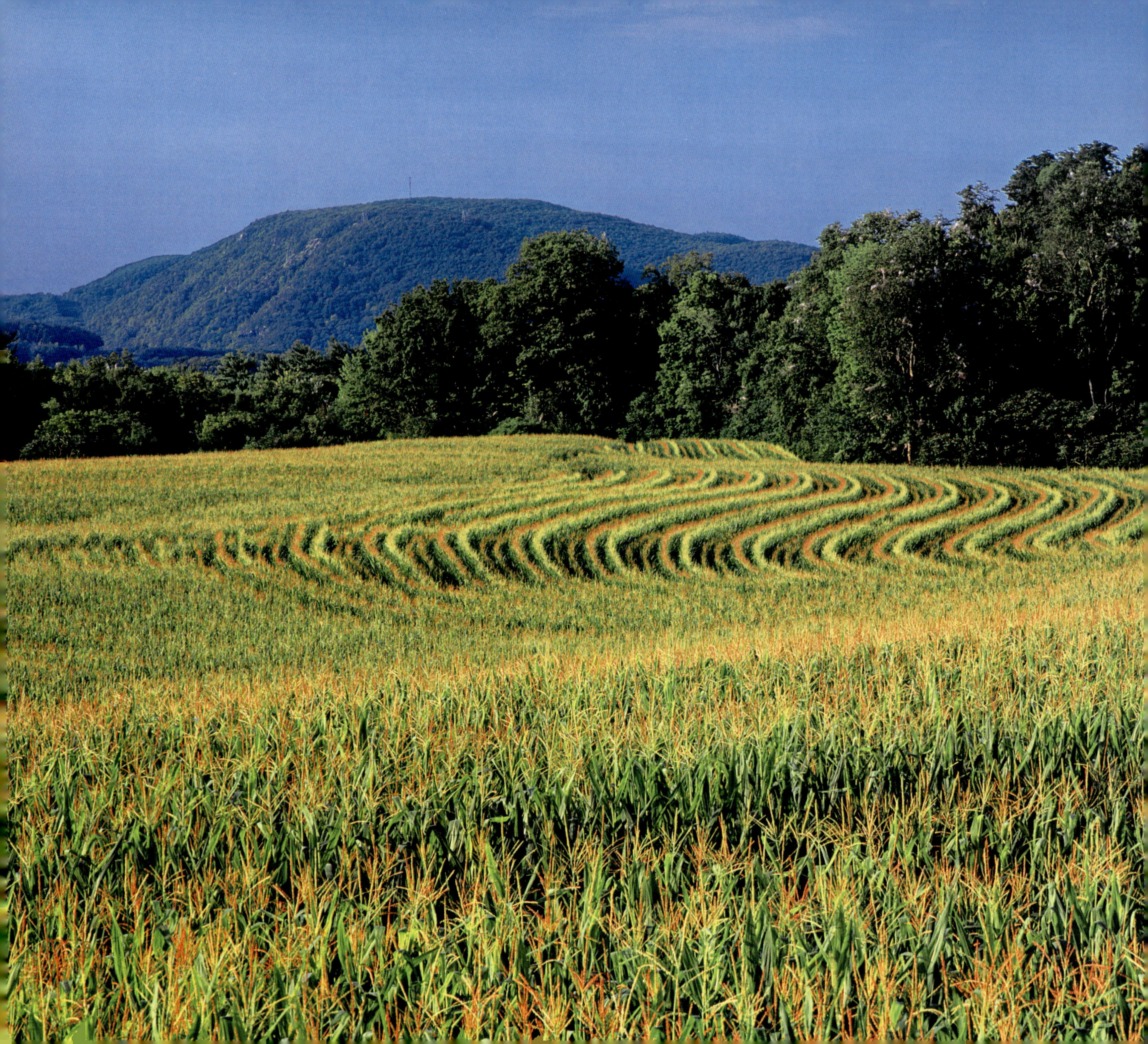

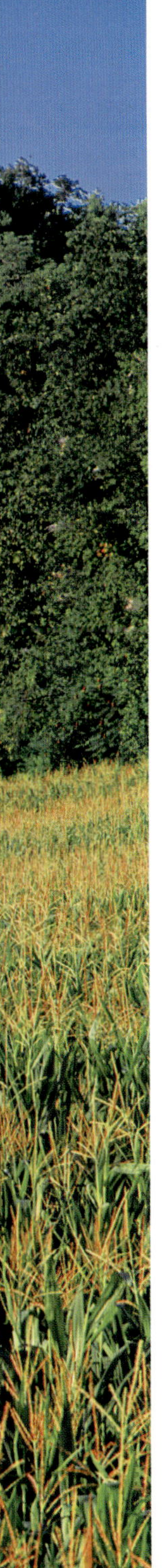

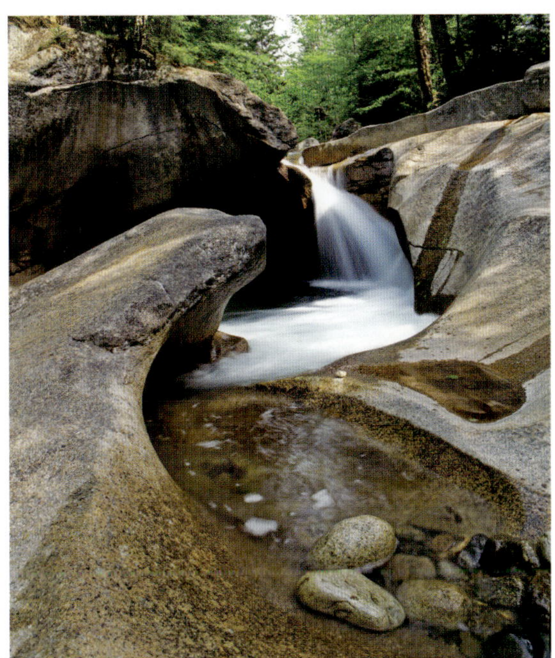

Left: The rushing waters of the Pemigewasset River sculpt modernist forms at Basin Falls in Franconia Notch State Park.

Far left: Curving cornfields outside the village of Walpole, in the lush Connecticut River Valley, hint at the peace and beauty that convinced iconic filmmaker Ken Burns to settle here.

Below: A misty calm settles over Bearcamp River. Surrounded by lakes and close to White Mountain ski areas, the greater Ossipee area was named for the Ossipee Indians and was once the site of a fort that protected the tribe.

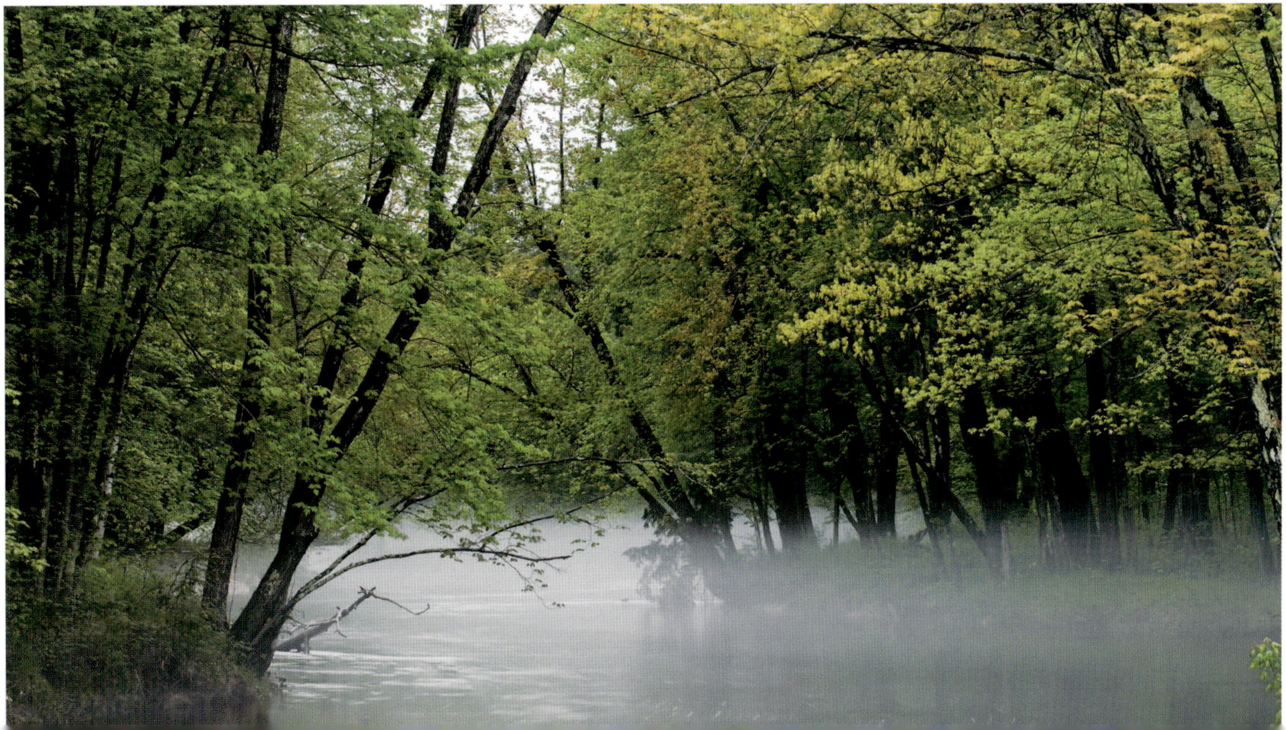

Right: A field of black-eyed Susans stretches to a distant tree line in Wentworth, the core of the Baker River Valley. Members of the sunflower family, these cheery native flowers are among the most popular wildflowers.

Far right: The Mad River flows through Waterville Valley in White Mountain National Forest, a playground for outdoor sports.

Below: Mount Major looks toward Lake Winnipesaukee, the state's largest lake. The popular Mount Major Trail, a 3.4-mile, dog-friendly loop, leads to a rocky summit perfect for picnics.

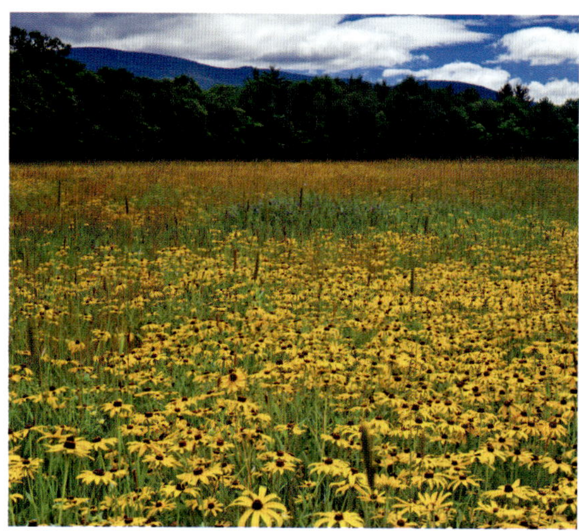

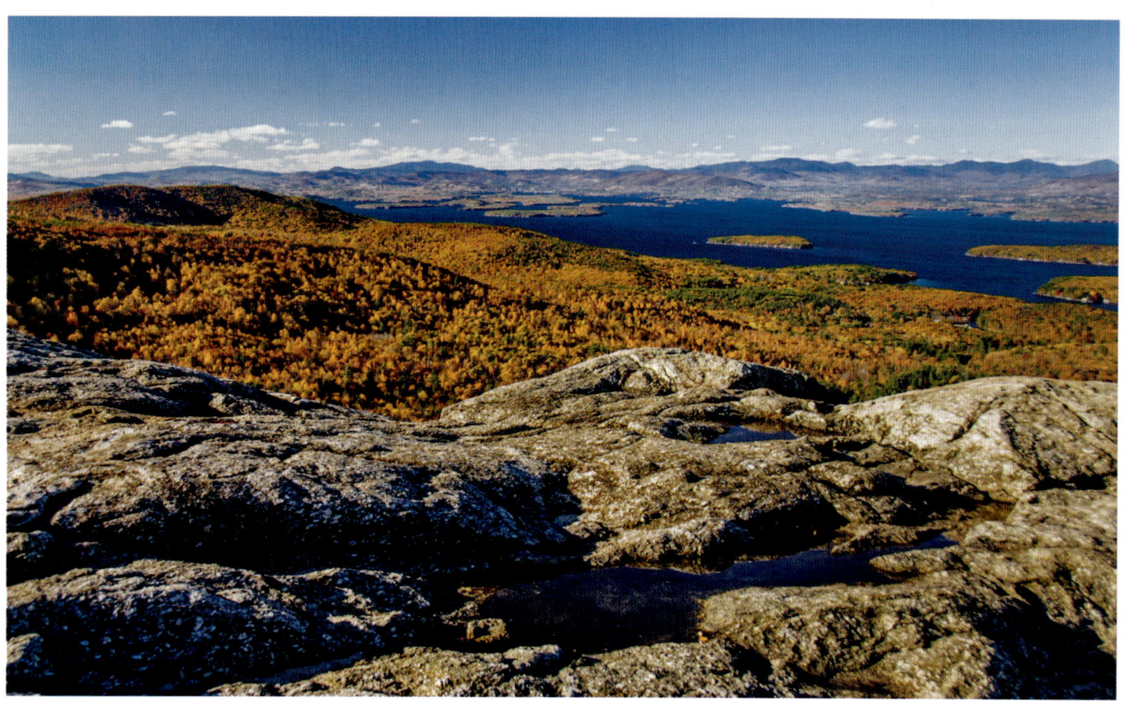

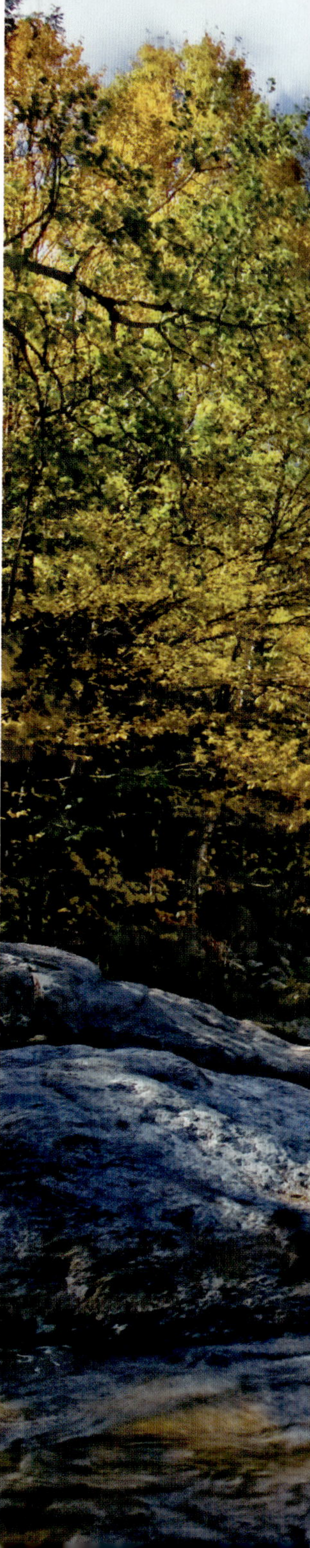

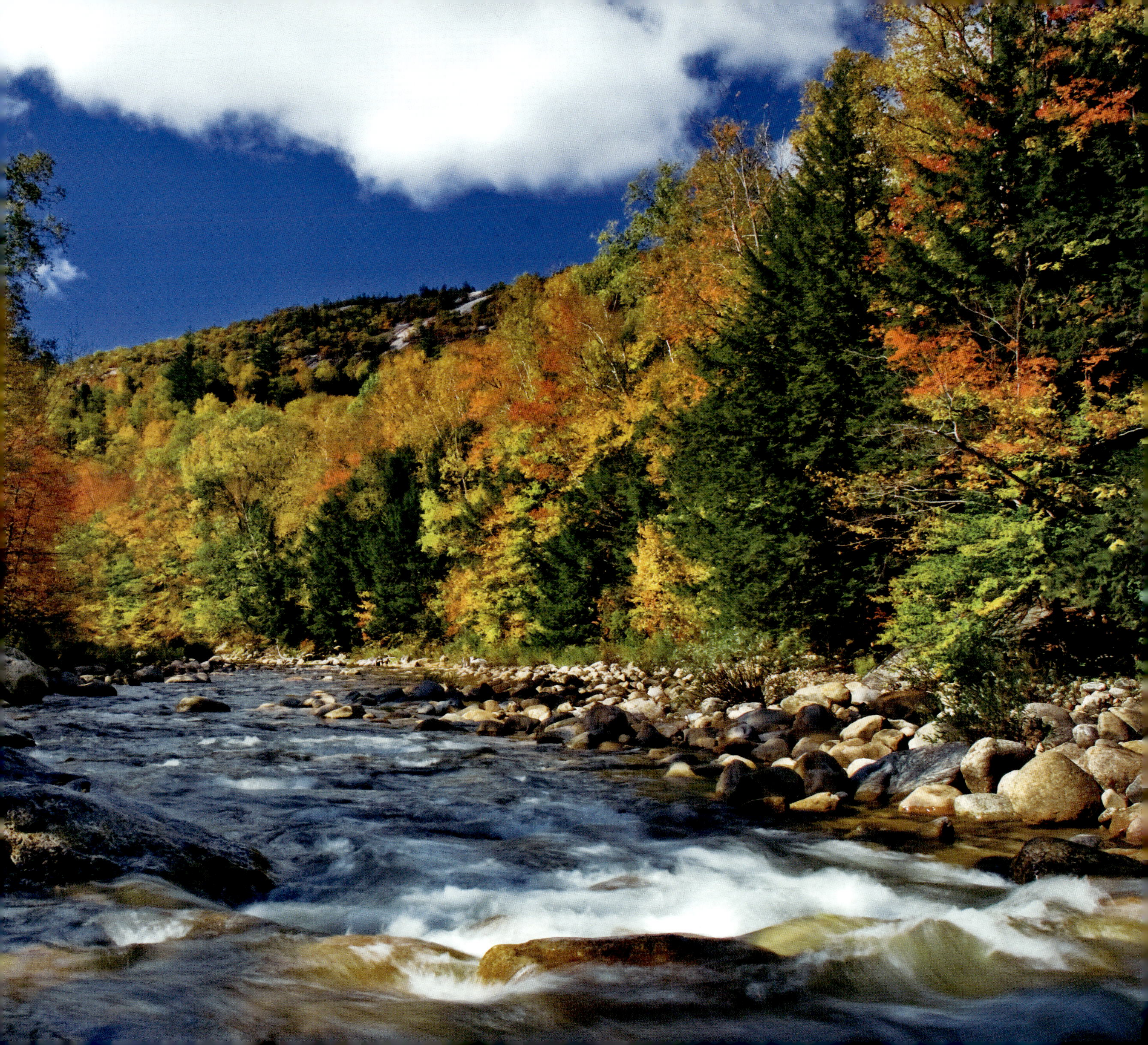

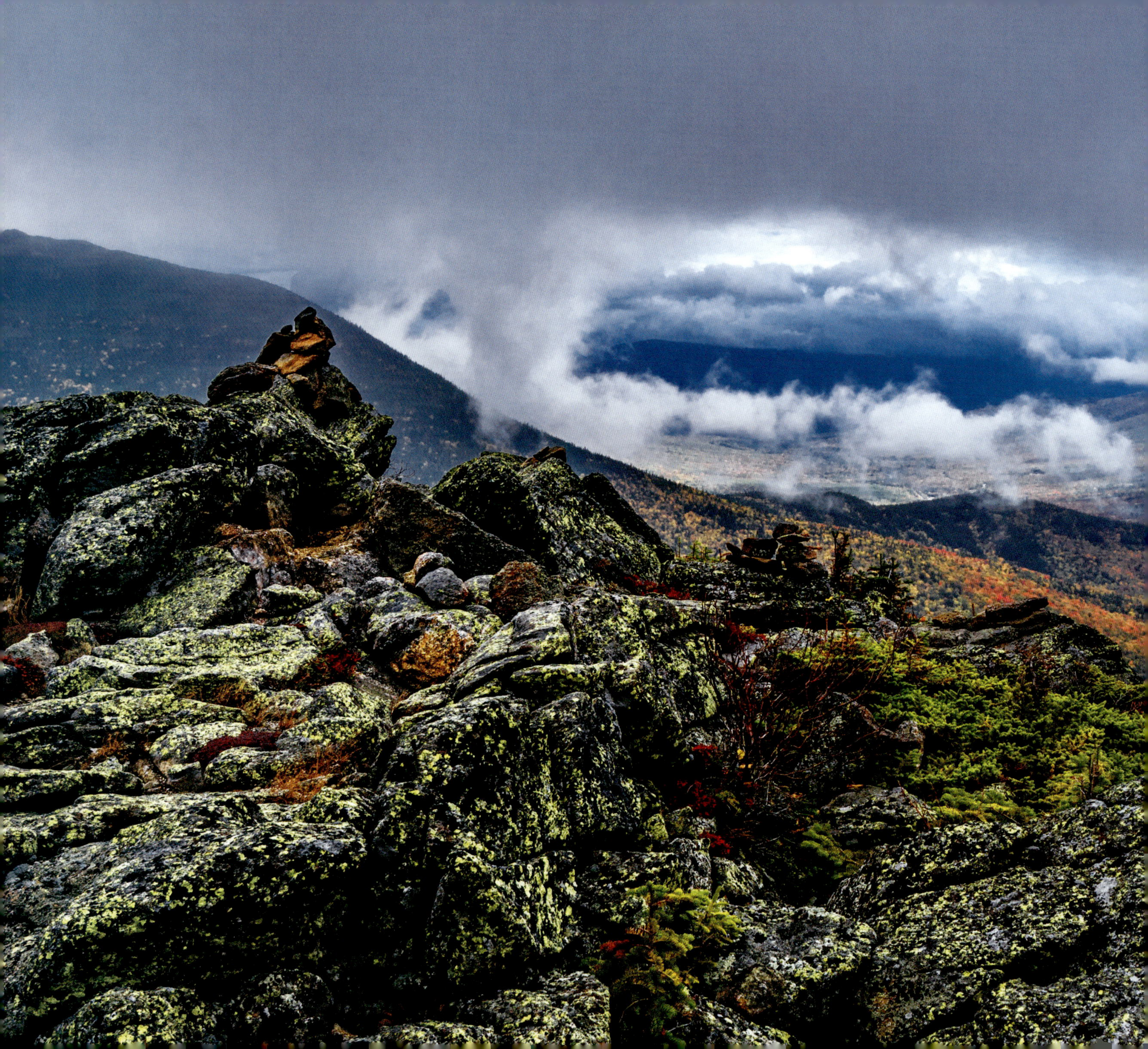

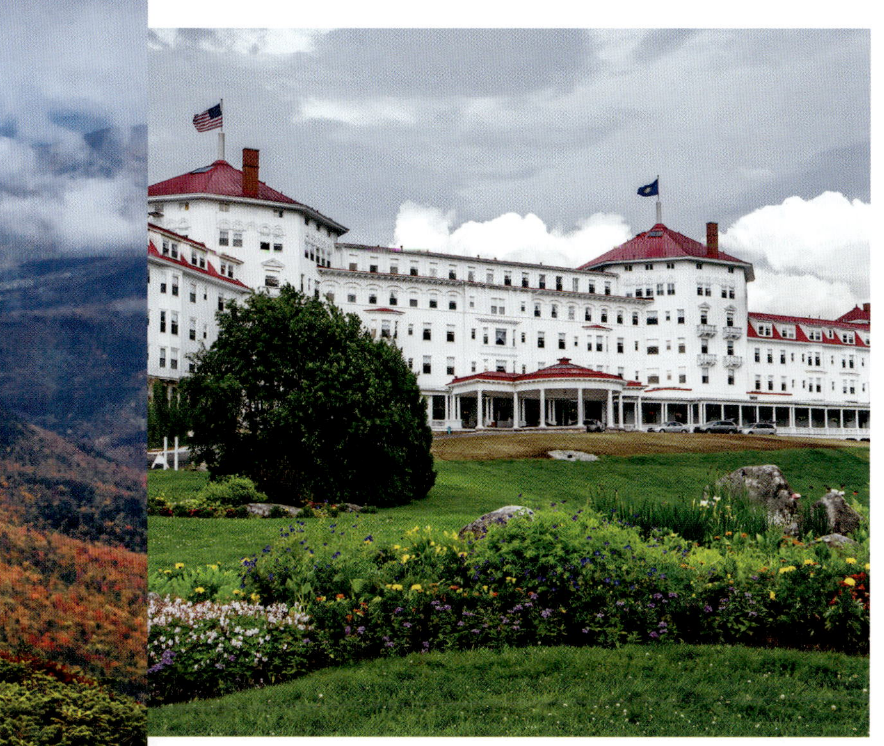

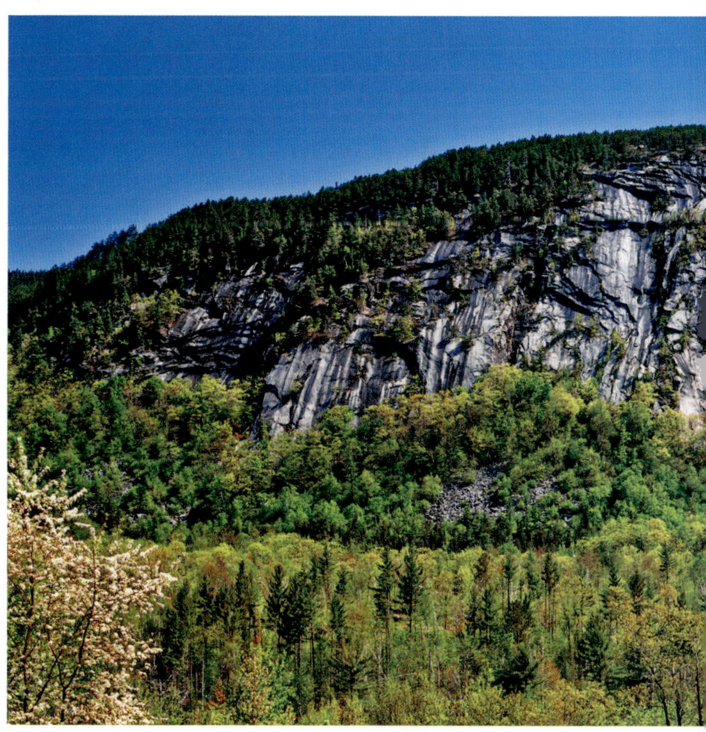

Above left: The most luxurious hotel of its day, the Omni Mount Washington Resort has welcomed distinguished guests since 1902. Its porch is one of the most famous in America, with mesmerizing views of Mount Washington.

Above right: Owls Head Ridge marks the ruggedly beautiful countryside around Warren, first settled in 1767, at the edge of White Mountain National Forest.

Left: The wild beauty of the Peabody River Valley, in Coös County, is a tapestry of color. The Mount Washington Valley tradition of trail cairns is well established here. More than merely decorative, these rock stacks are important trail indicators, maintained by the Appalachian Mountain Club and White Mountain National Forest staff.

Facing page: Color drenches Silver Cascades in Crawford Notch State Park. The Conway Scenic Railroad runs right through Crawford Notch, dangling from the hillsides, and is widely considered to be one of the most dramatic train rides in New England.

Right: Former textile mills in Manchester have been converted to upscale restaurants and attractions like the Millyard Museum, which pays tribute to the city's mill history. The SEE Science Center, in the same building, is home to the largest LEGO model in the country: three million LEGOs recreating Manchester's Amoskeag Millyard.

Below right: Weathered barns—a New Hampshire specialty—are especially pretty in fall, the warm wood echoing autumn's fiery colors.

Below: Trains climb mountains too, but the Mount Washington Cog Railway was the first to do so. The railway first brought the engine *Old Peppersass* to the peak in 1869, climbing three miles up the steepest tracks in the United States to the 6,288-foot summit. The newest locomotive, *Wajo Nanatasis* (Abenaki for "mountain hummingbird"), also blazes an innovative trail: its engine is biodiesel.

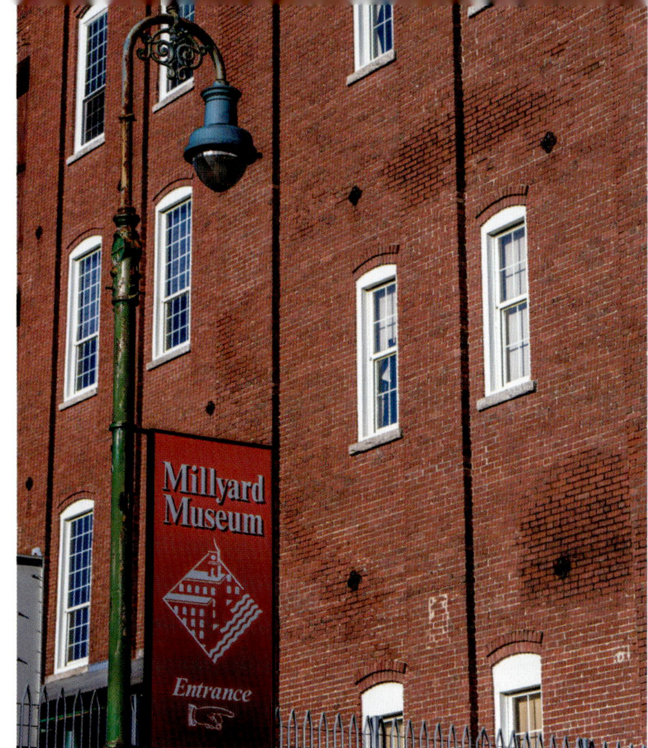

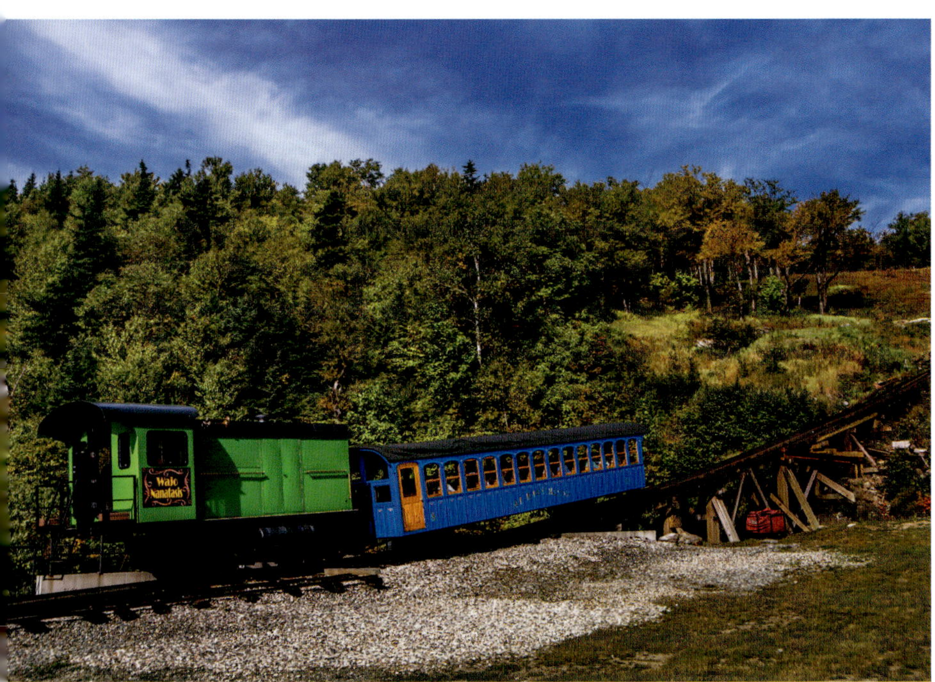

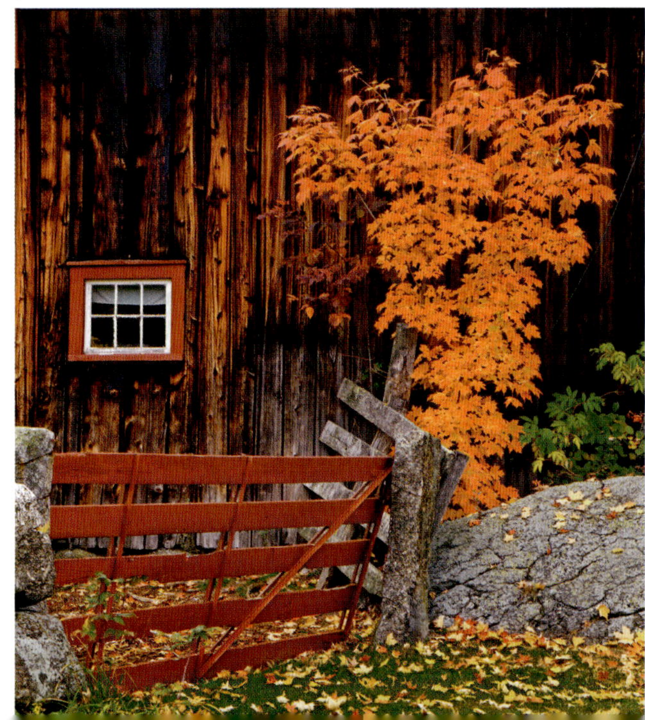

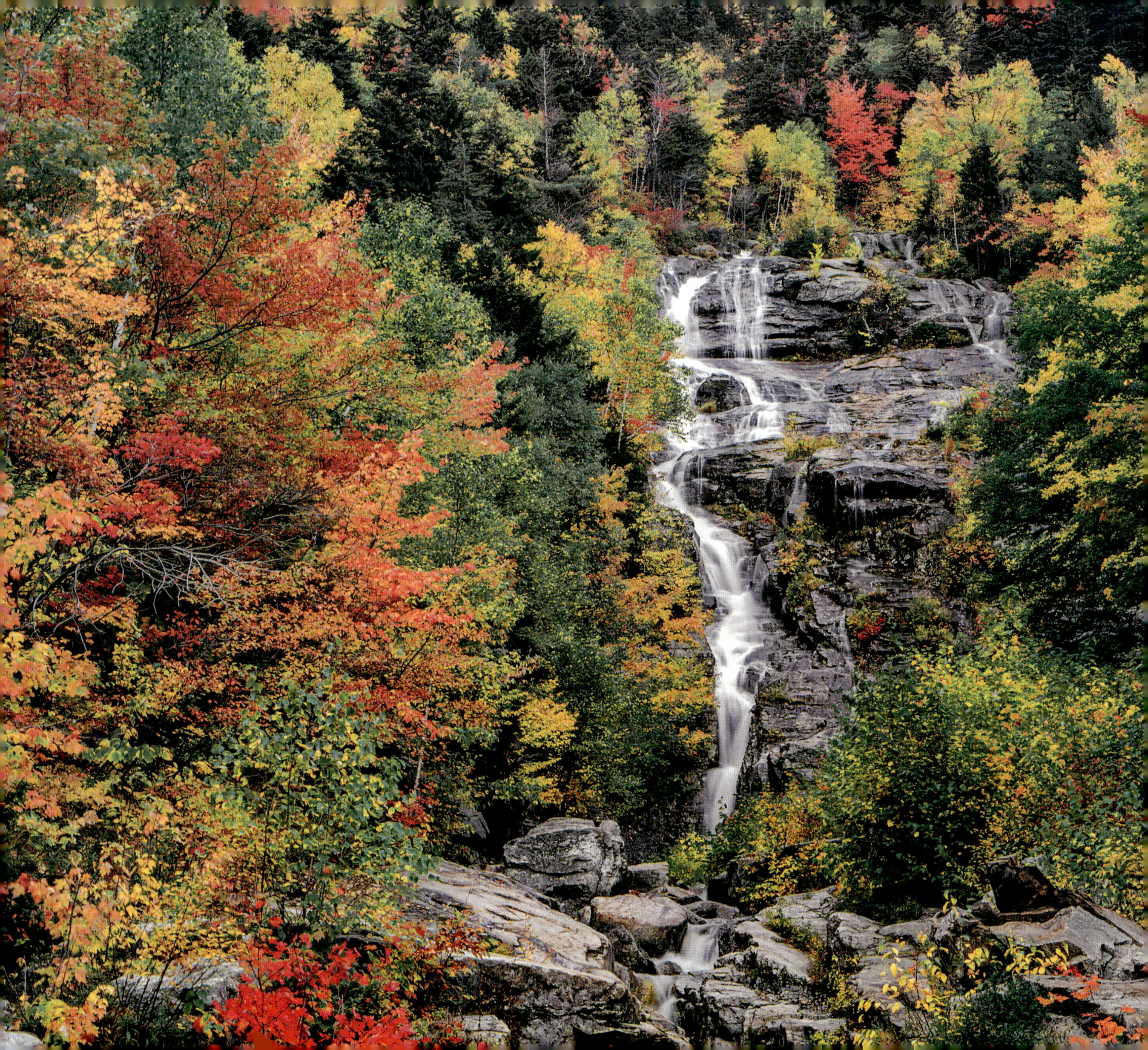

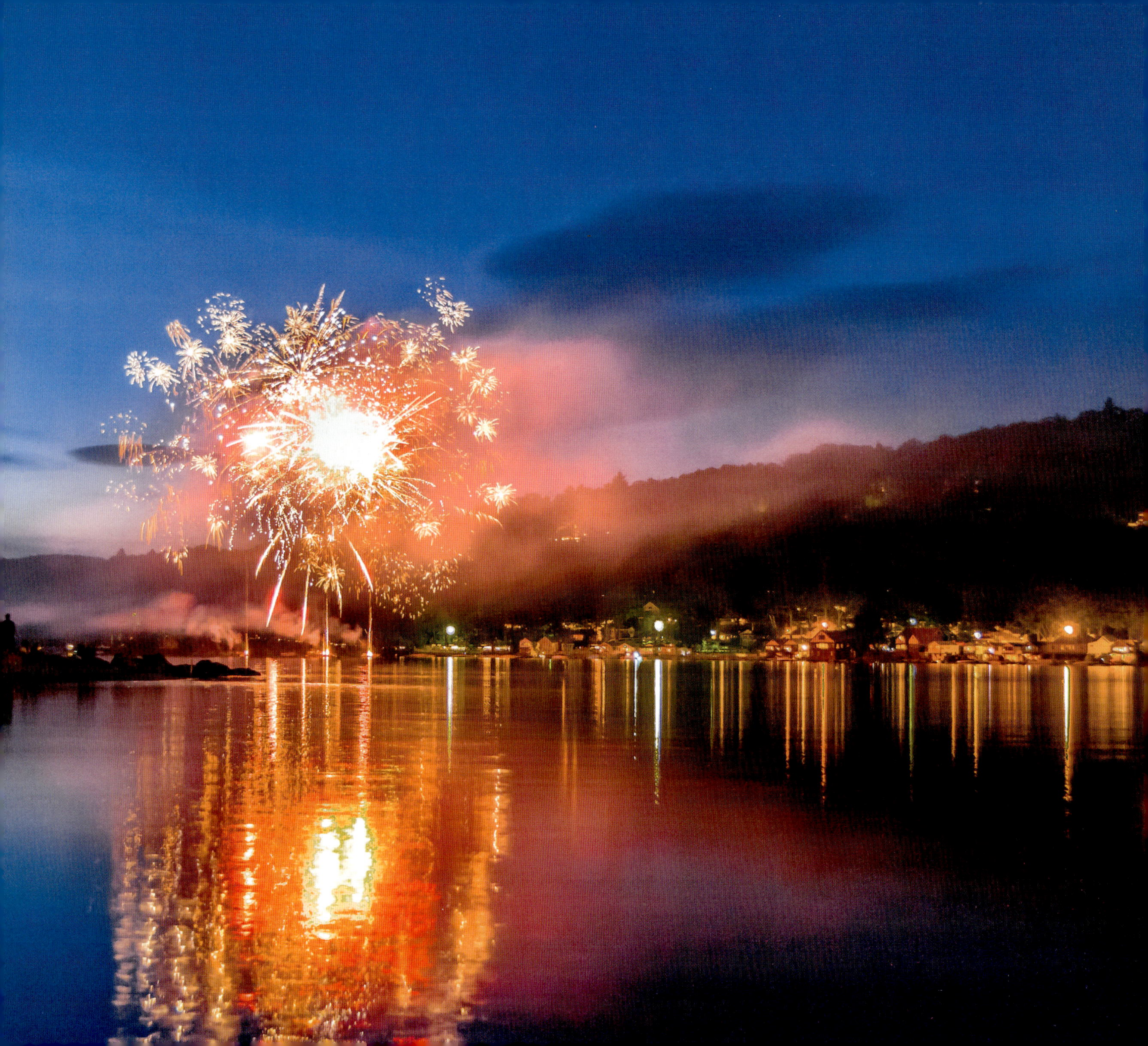

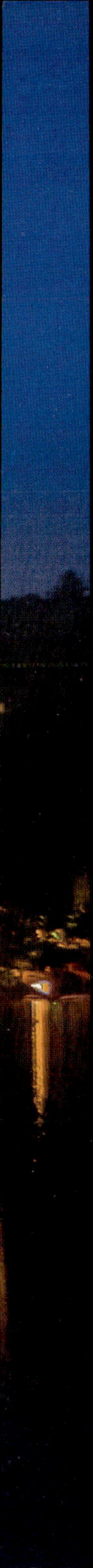

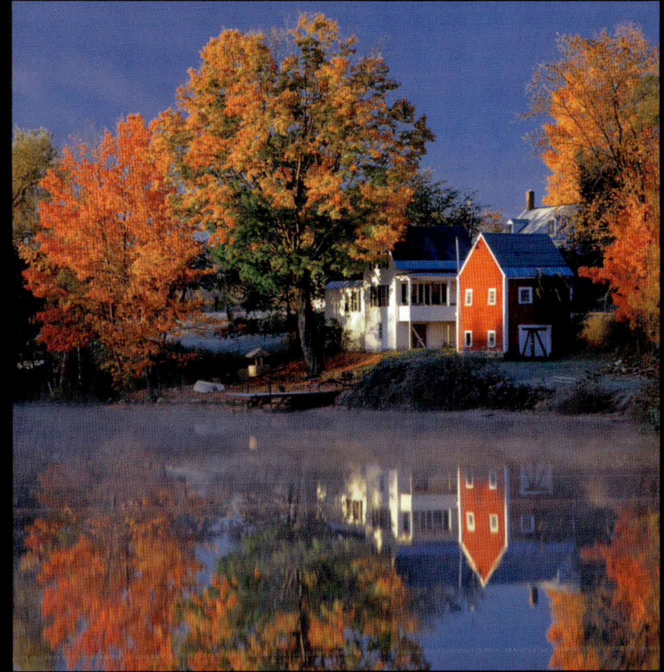

Left: A red barn pairs with fall foliage in East Andover in the Merrimack Valley, where the countryside is bounded by a triangle of the state's three major cities: Concord, Manchester, and Nashua.

Far left: Fireworks fly over the glacial depths of Newfound Lake, a pristine body of water on the western edge of the Lakes Region.

Below: Hollyhocks frame the home of the celebrated Irish-born American sculptor Augustus Saint-Gaudens, who lived from 1848 to 1907. He is known for such works as *Standing Lincoln* in Chicago, *Memorial to Robert Gould Shaw* in Boston, and an innovative Double Eagle gold coin. Saint-Gaudens National Historic Site preserves Saint-Gaudens' home and studio in Cornish.

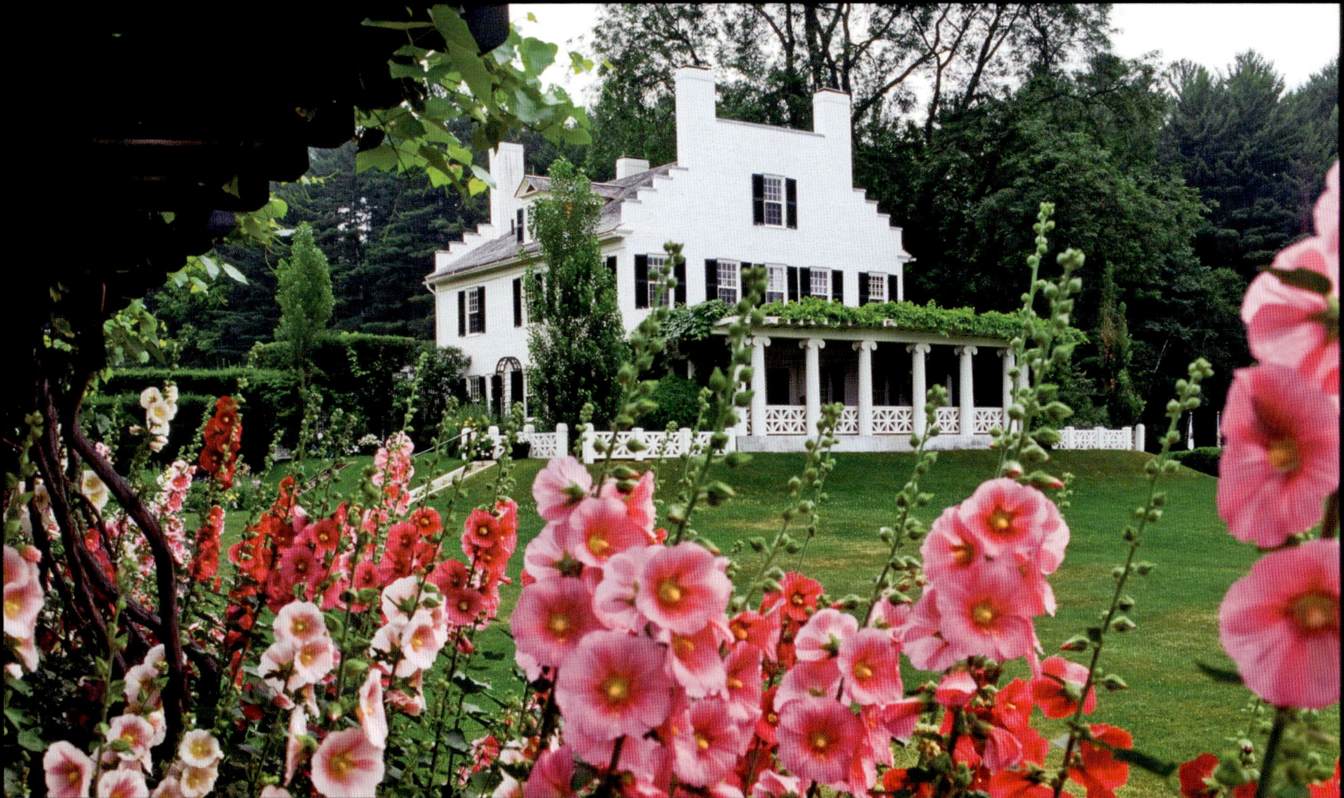

Right: A monument to preservationists, the 1823 knitting factory Belknap Mill has found new life as a museum and art gallery on the banks of the Winnipesaukee River in Laconia.

Far right: Built in the mid-1800s, the Flume Covered Bridge spans the rumbling Pemigewasset River. It is a gateway to the magnificent Flume Gorge, an 800-foot gorge spilling over with waterfalls and lined with vertiginous footpaths.

Below: New Hampshire's tumbled coastline is short but sweet. Odiorne Point State Park's Seacoast Science Center offers marine exhibits inside and geology lessons outside.

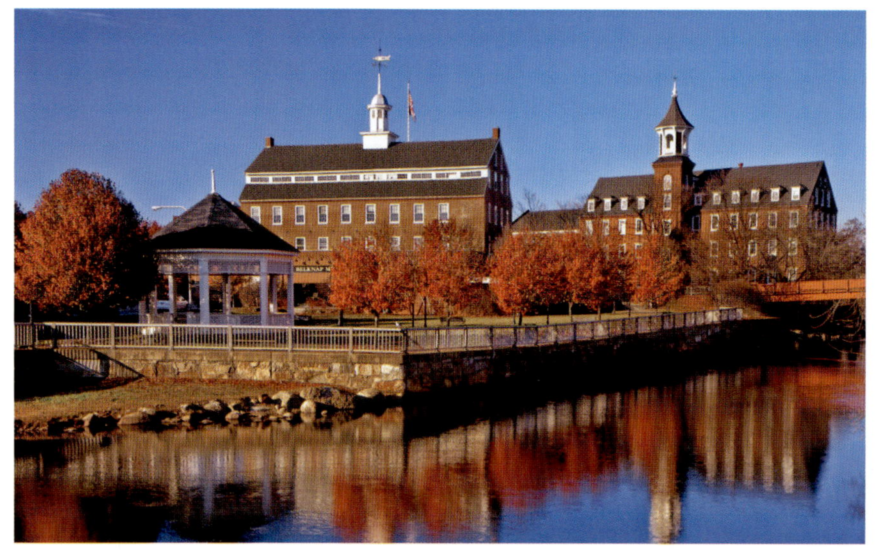

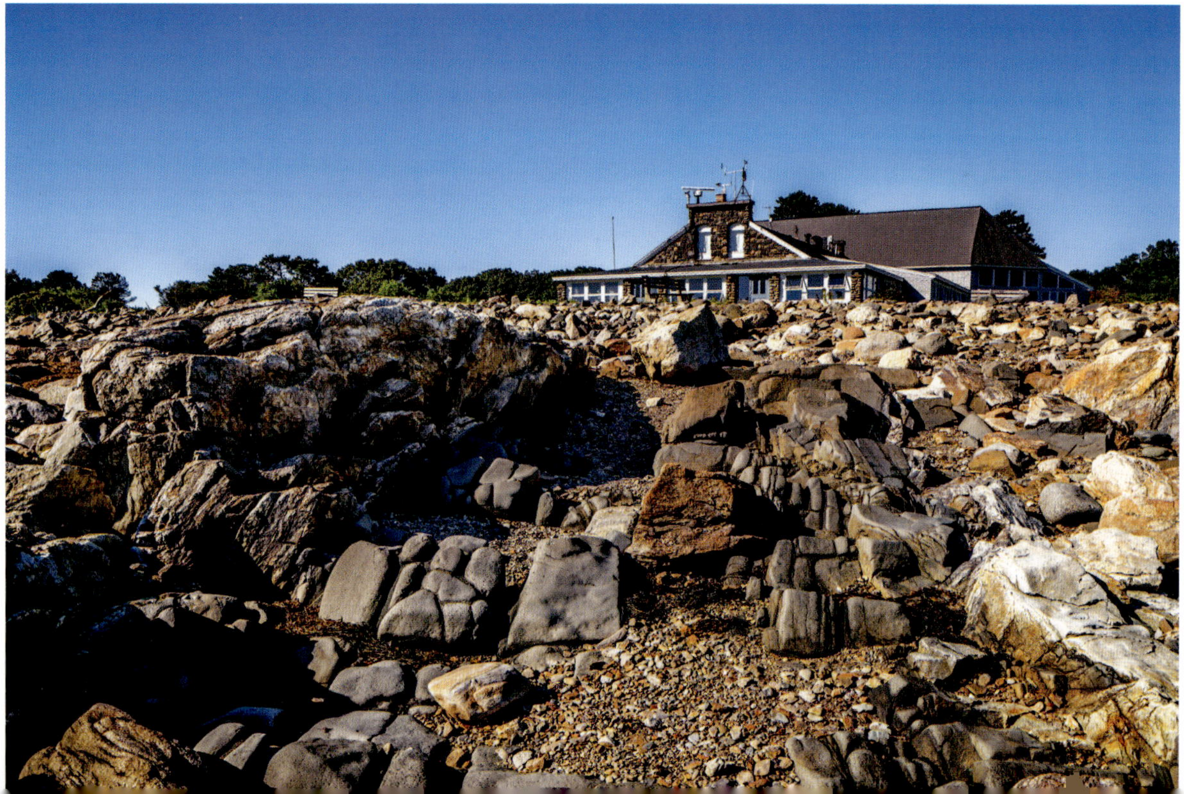

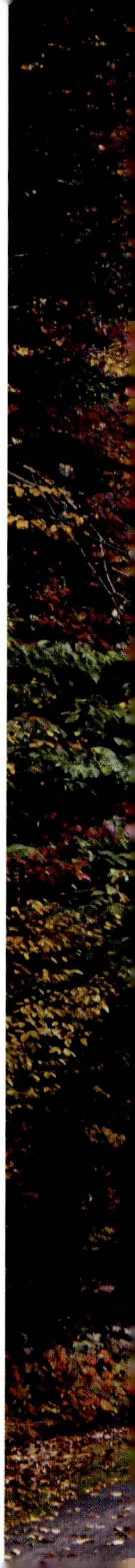

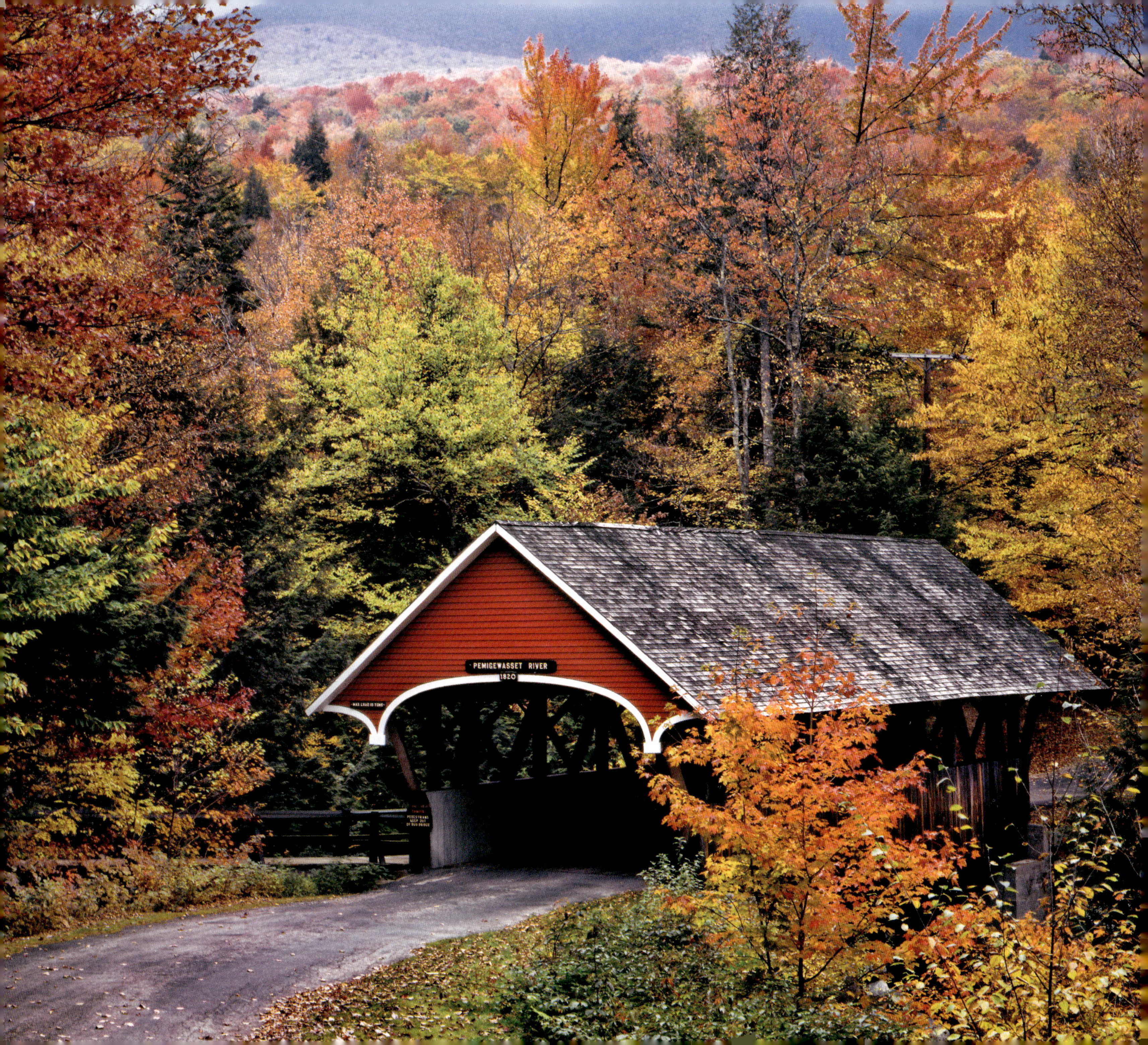
PEMIGEWASSET RIVER
1820

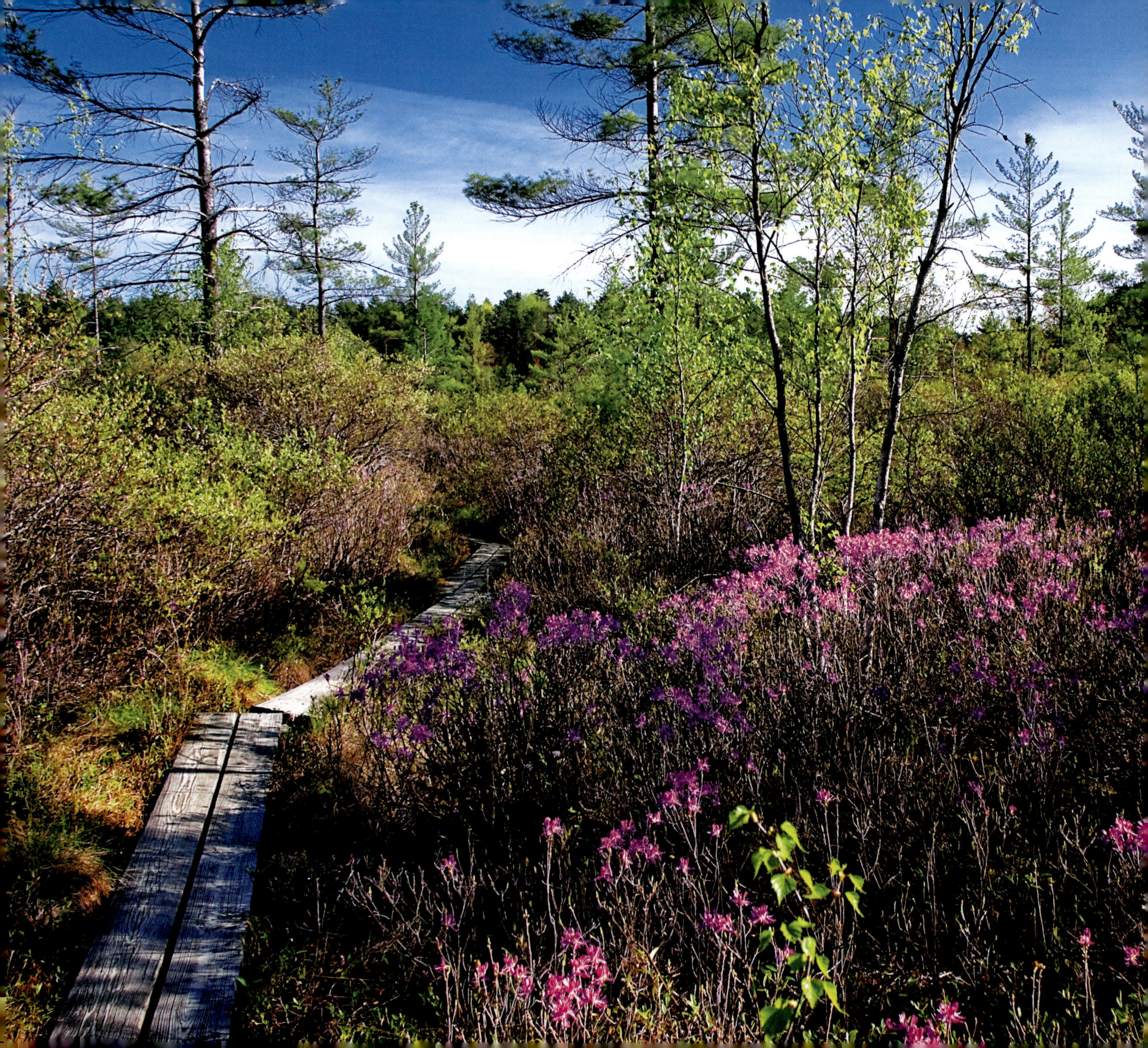

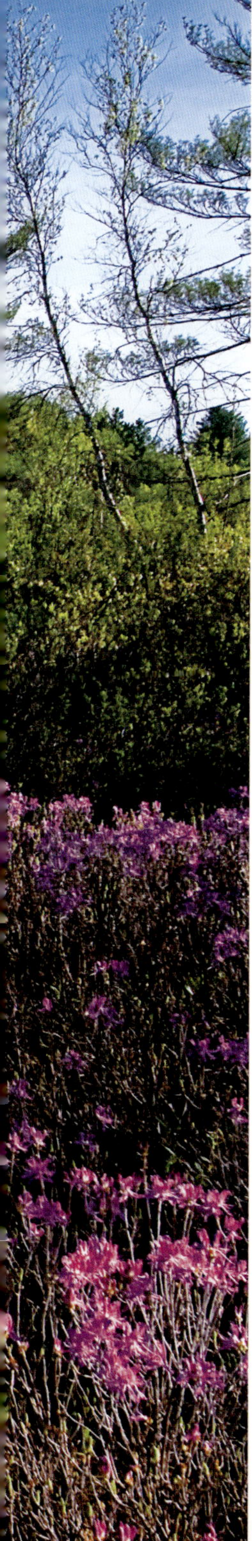

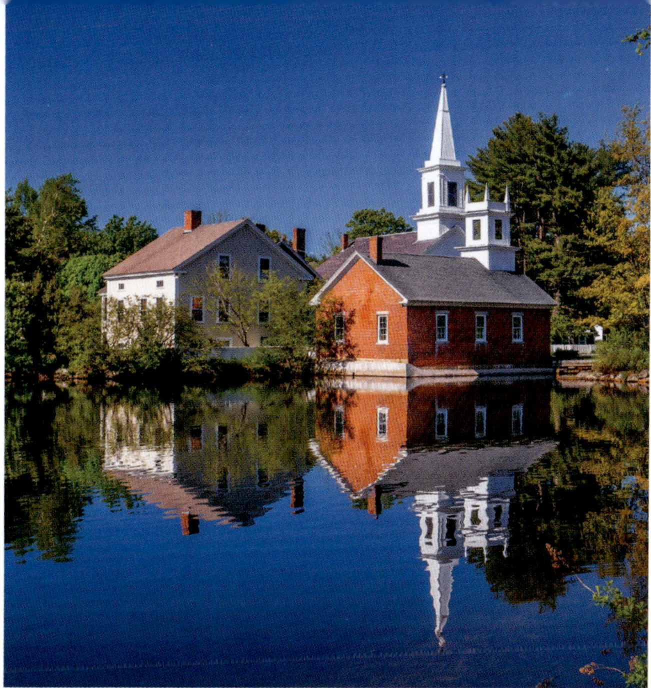

Left: A pretty brick library sits in the picturesque nineteenth-century mill village of Harrisville, in the heart of the Monadnock Region.

Far left: A weathered wooden trail meanders through Ponemah Bog in Amherst. Formed by glacial ice and thousands of years of plant life, kettle hole bogs such as this provide homes for unusual plants, mosses, and wildlife, combining to create an otherworldly effect.

Below: Lilacs bloom near an iconic barn in Hudson, along the Merrimack River, just five minutes from the city of Nashua. Purple lilac is the state flower, and the state's oldest bushes, from 1750, grow at the Wentworth-Coolidge Mansion in Portsmouth.

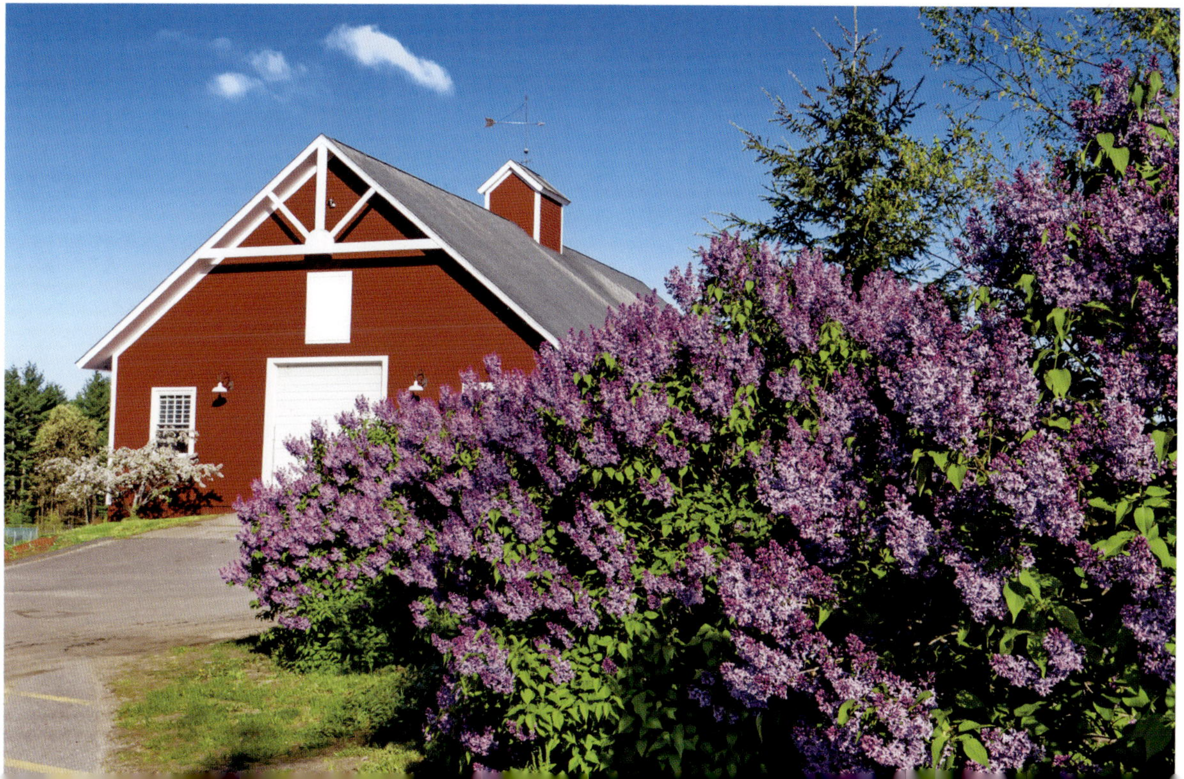

Right: Center Sandwich enjoys a reputation as one of the best places to watch foliage burst into color, but early spring has its own gentle appeal. Such beauty has inspired local and visiting artists since the town was founded in 1763.

Far right: Brook trout abound in the Upper Ammonoosuc River, which gets its start on Mount Washington, at Lakes of the Clouds, and rolls through the hamlet of Stark.

Below: Spring thaw adds to the swift-running Ammonoosuc as it pours through Lower Ammonoosuc Falls and cascades over layers of bedrock outside the town of Carroll.

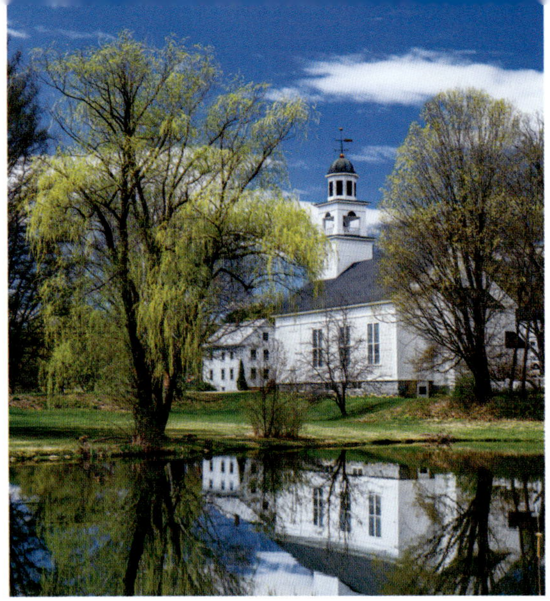

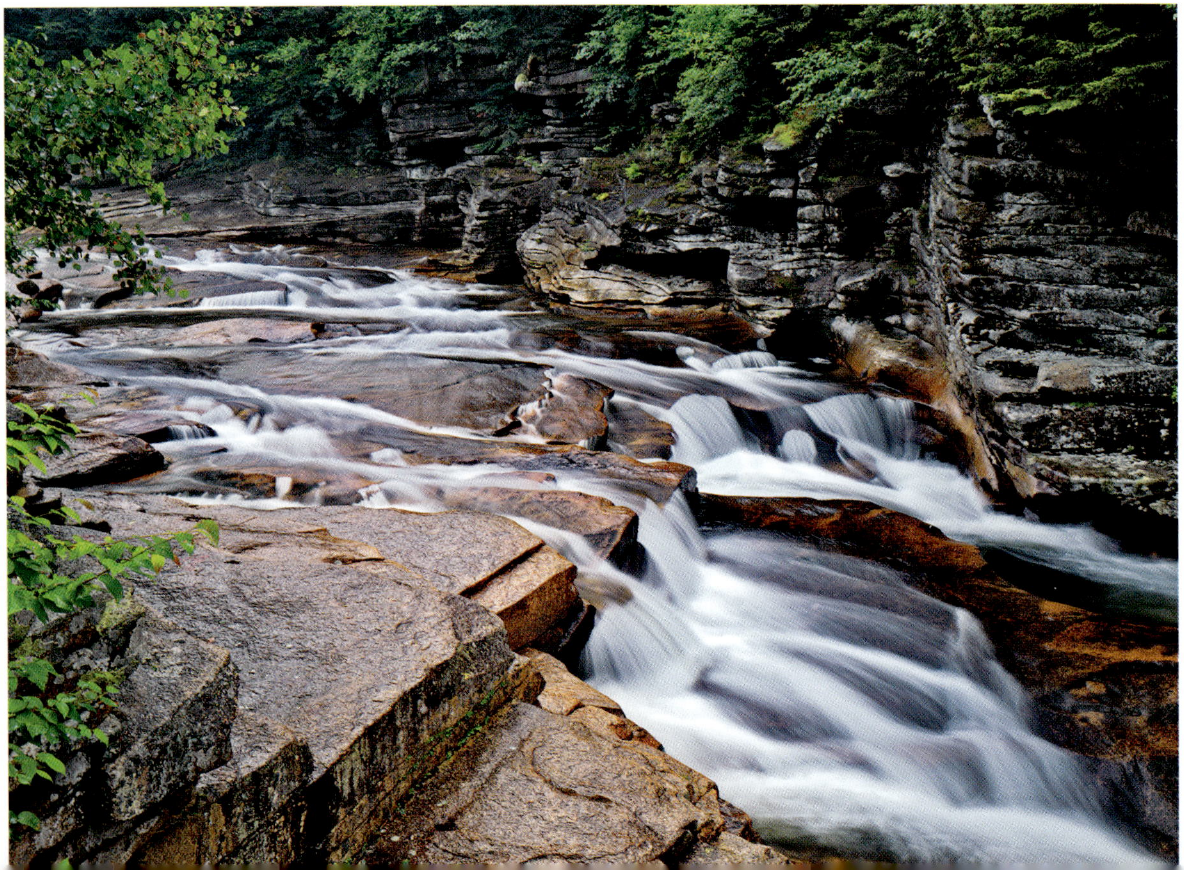

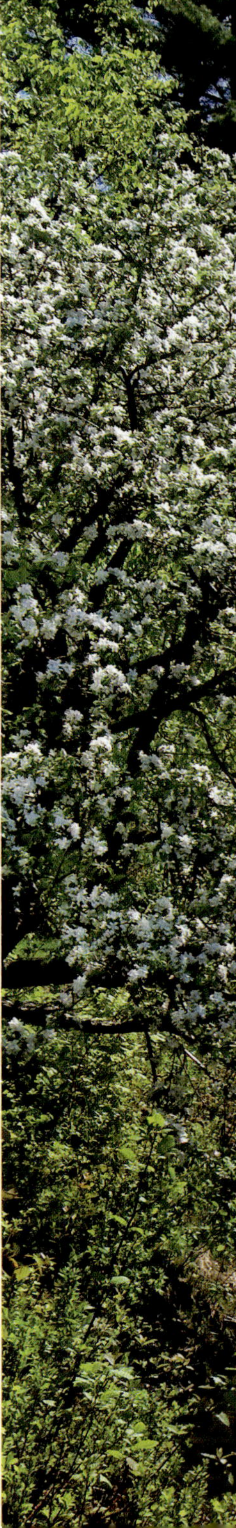

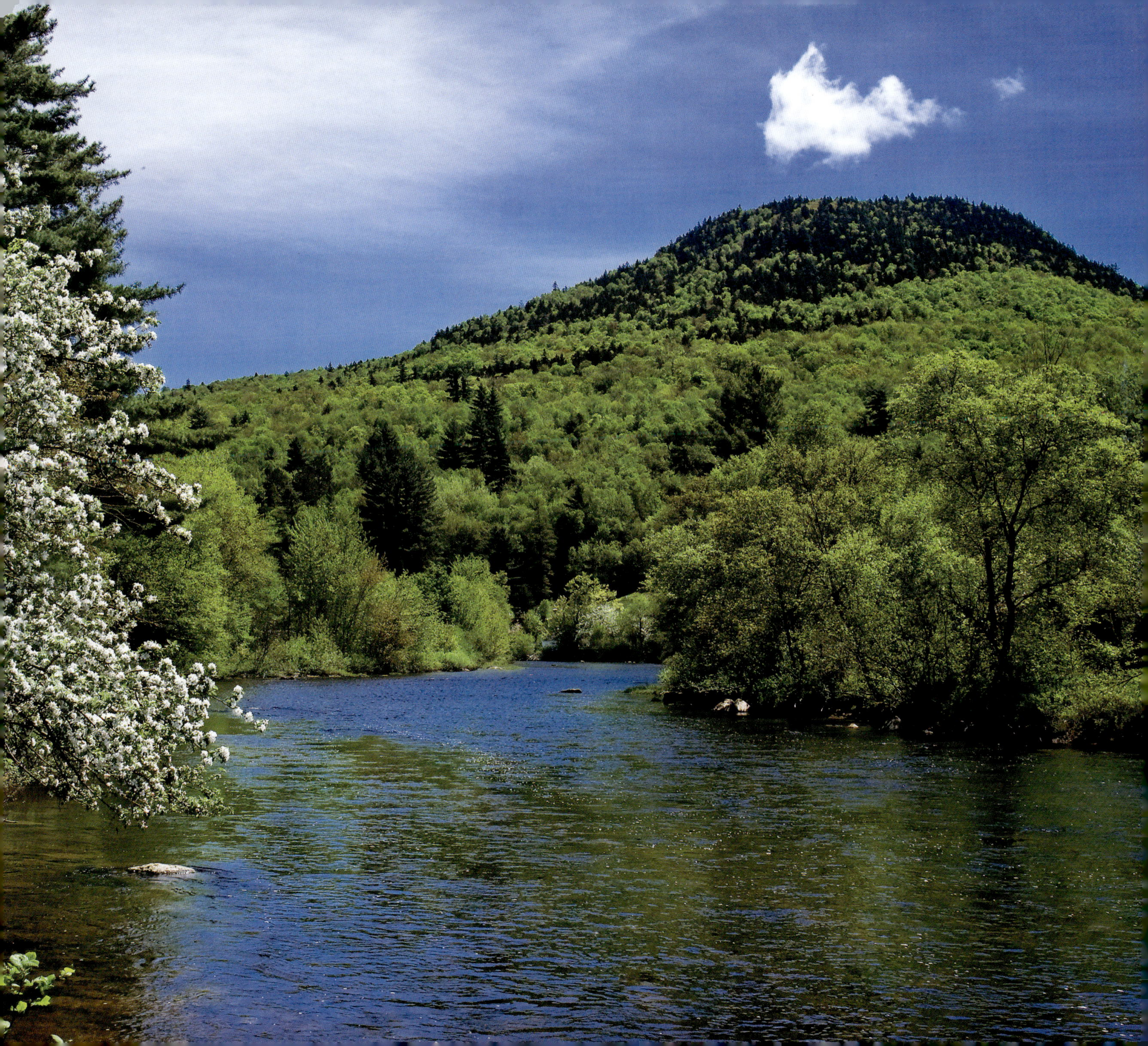

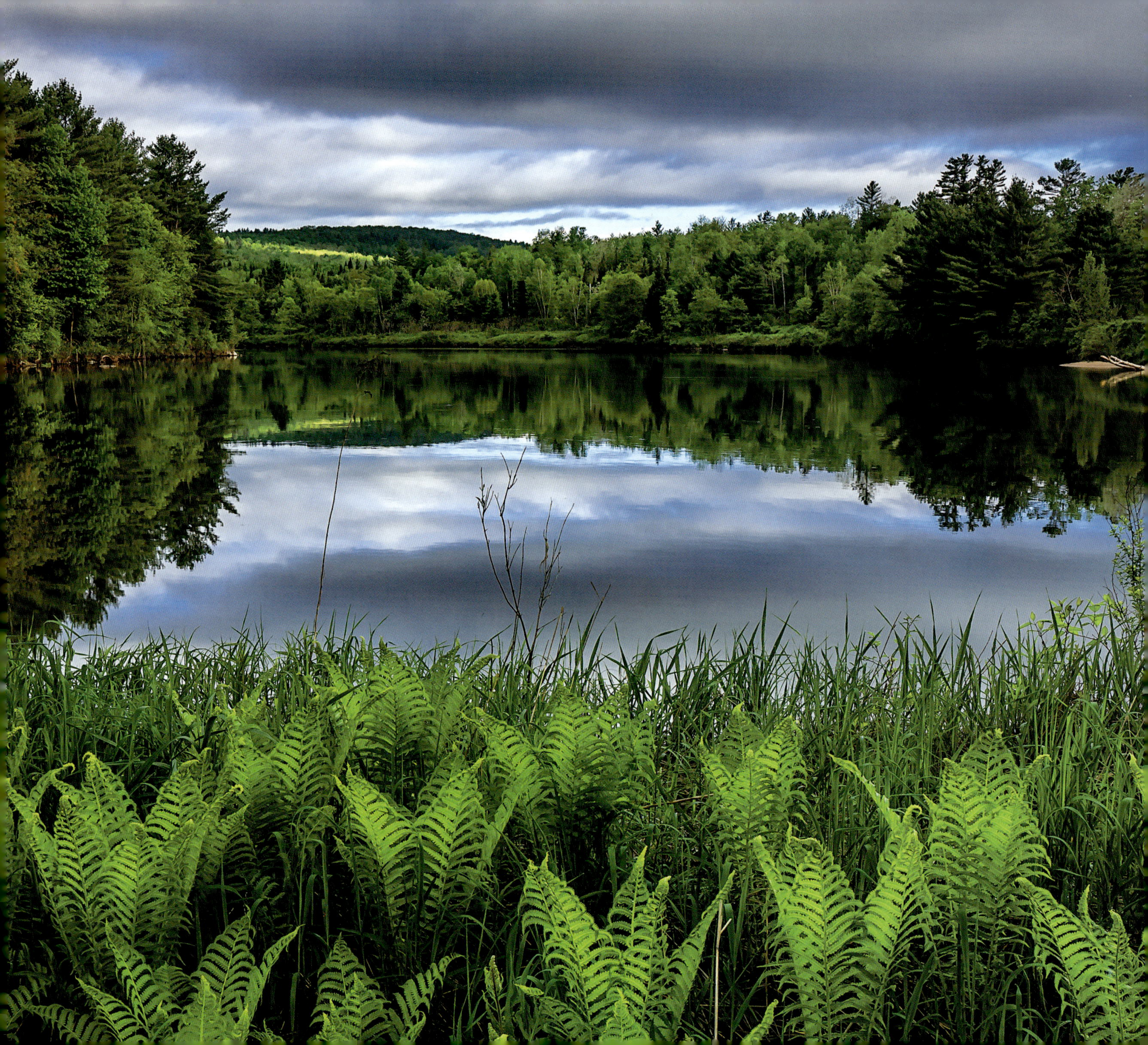

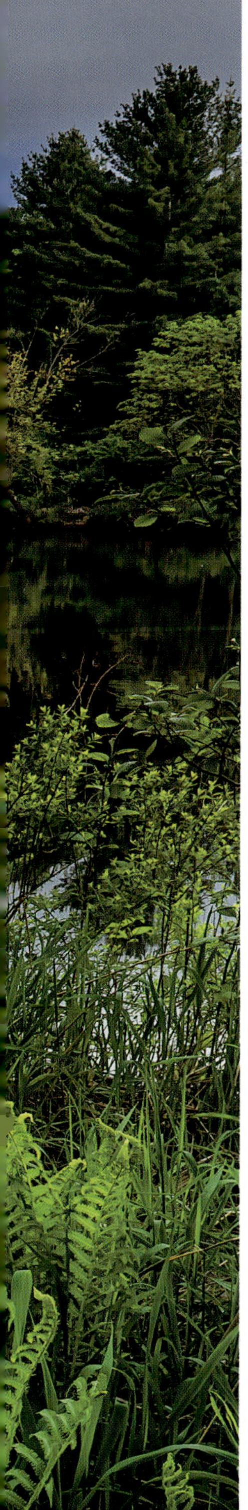

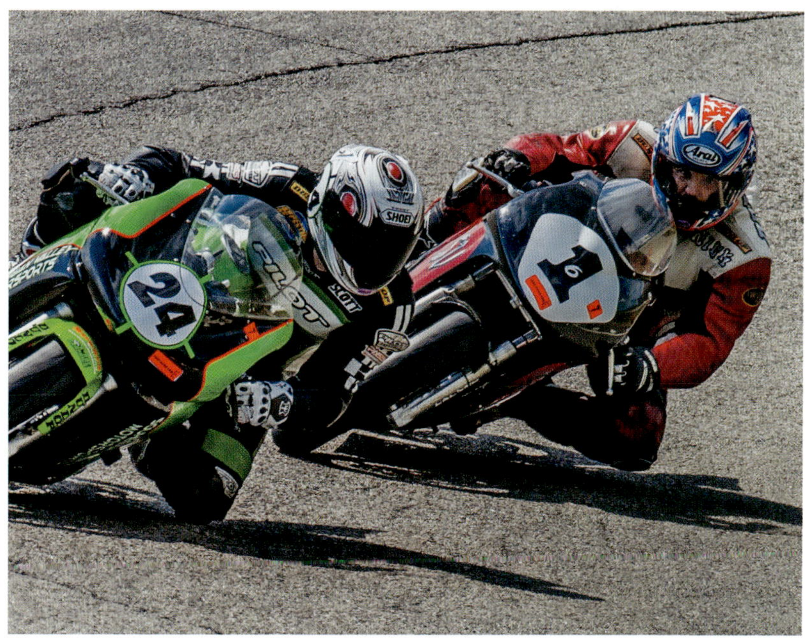

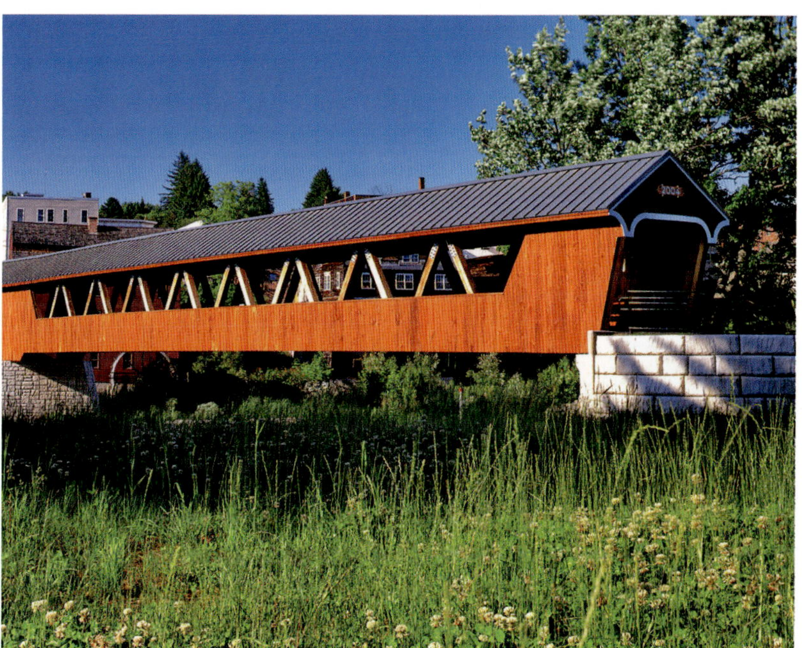

Above left: Riders lean into the curve at the Loudon Road Race Series (LRRS) at the New Hampshire Motor Speedway. The state's epicenter for motor sports, Loudon hosts a range of NASCAR and road racing events.

Left: A pretty newcomer to the covered bridge scene, Littleton's 300-foot bridge, near Main Street, was built in 2004 across the Ammonoosuc River.

Far left: North of the White Mountains, a perfect spring day in Dalton is reflected in the Connecticut River edged with new ferns.

Right: Sunlight filters through fog on the Pemigewasset River as it snakes through the Lakes Region near New Hampton.

Far right: Snowcaps on Mount Washington and the Presidential Range stand out against a cloudless blue sky.

Below: From its home in Boothbay Harbor, Maine, the schooner *Spirit of Massachusetts*, built in 1984, hearkens back to the days when fleets of tall ships sailed past the Fort Constitution lighthouse in the Piscataqua River.

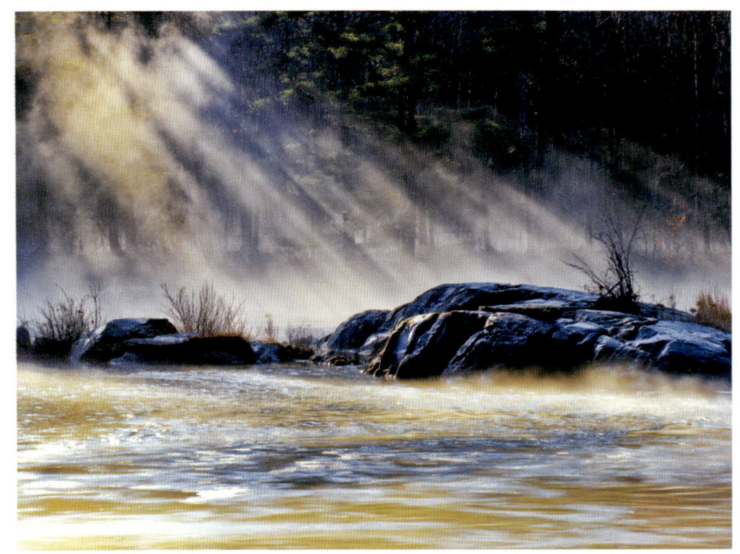

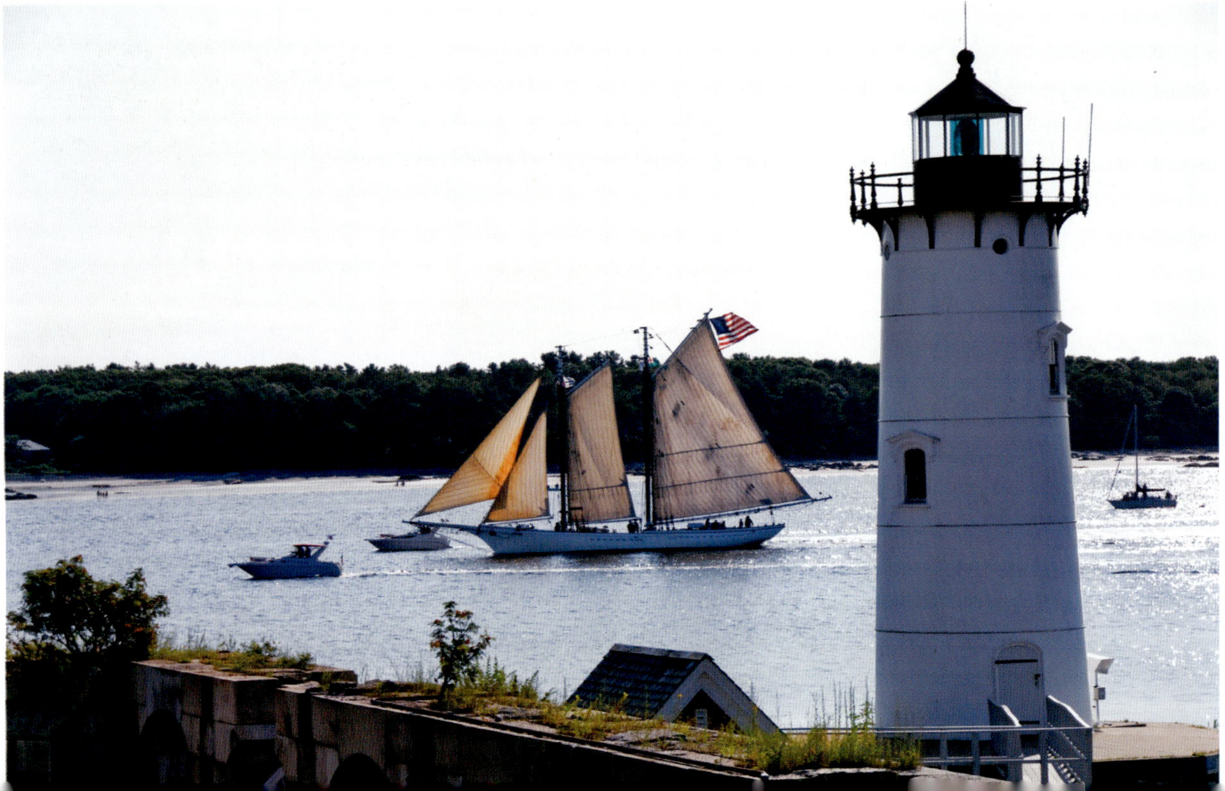

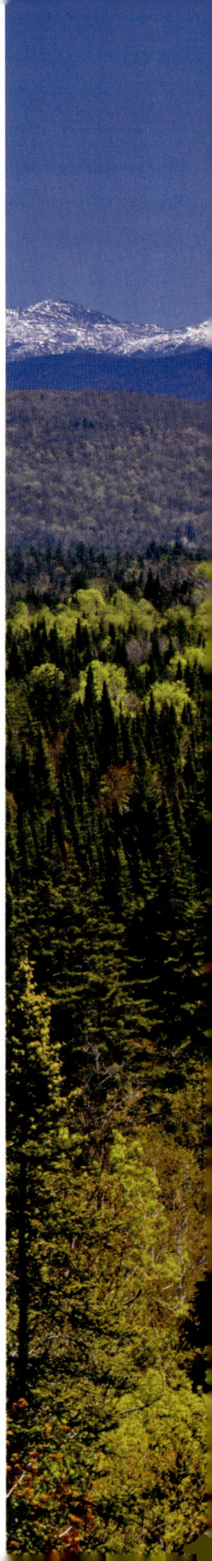

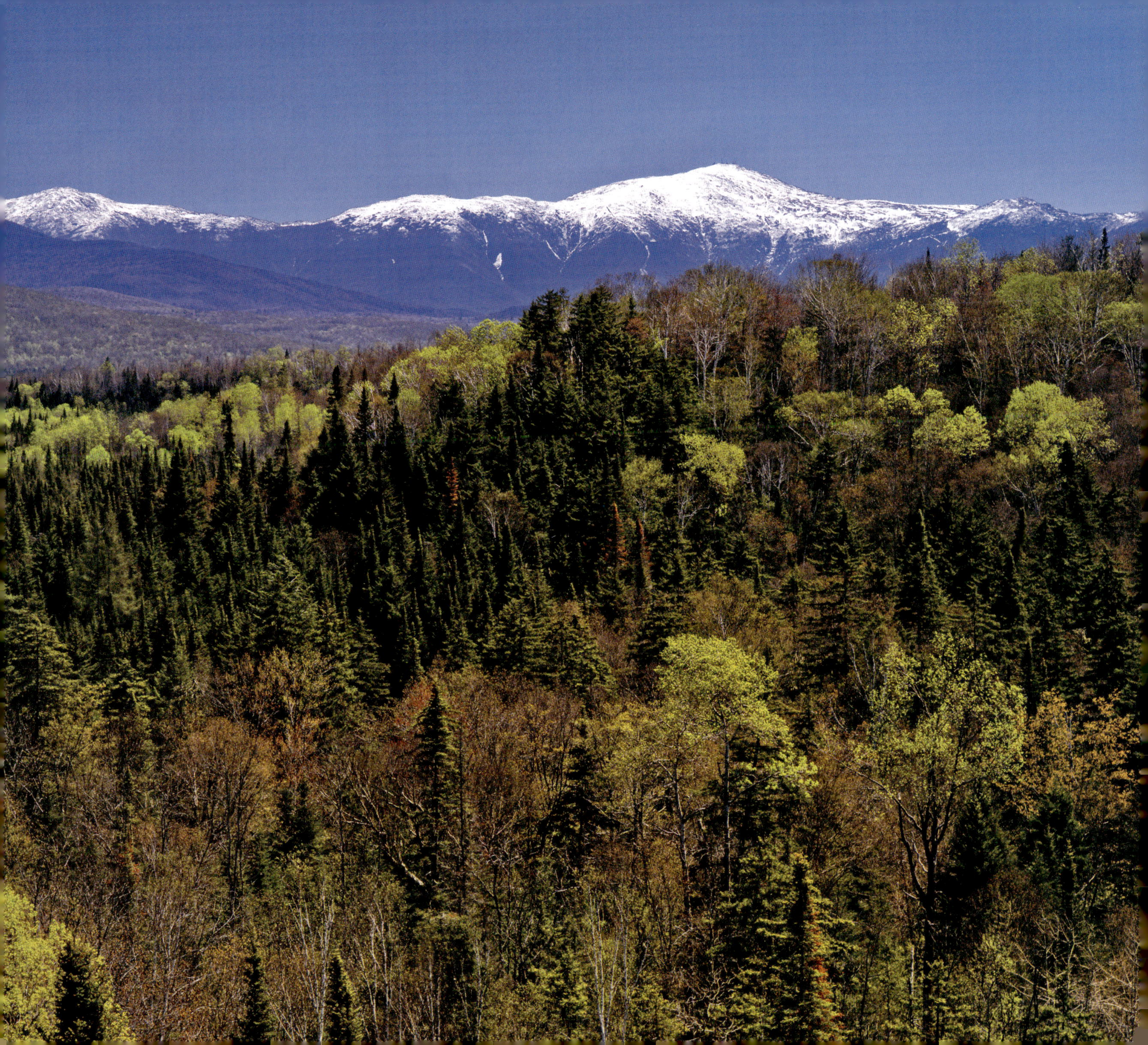

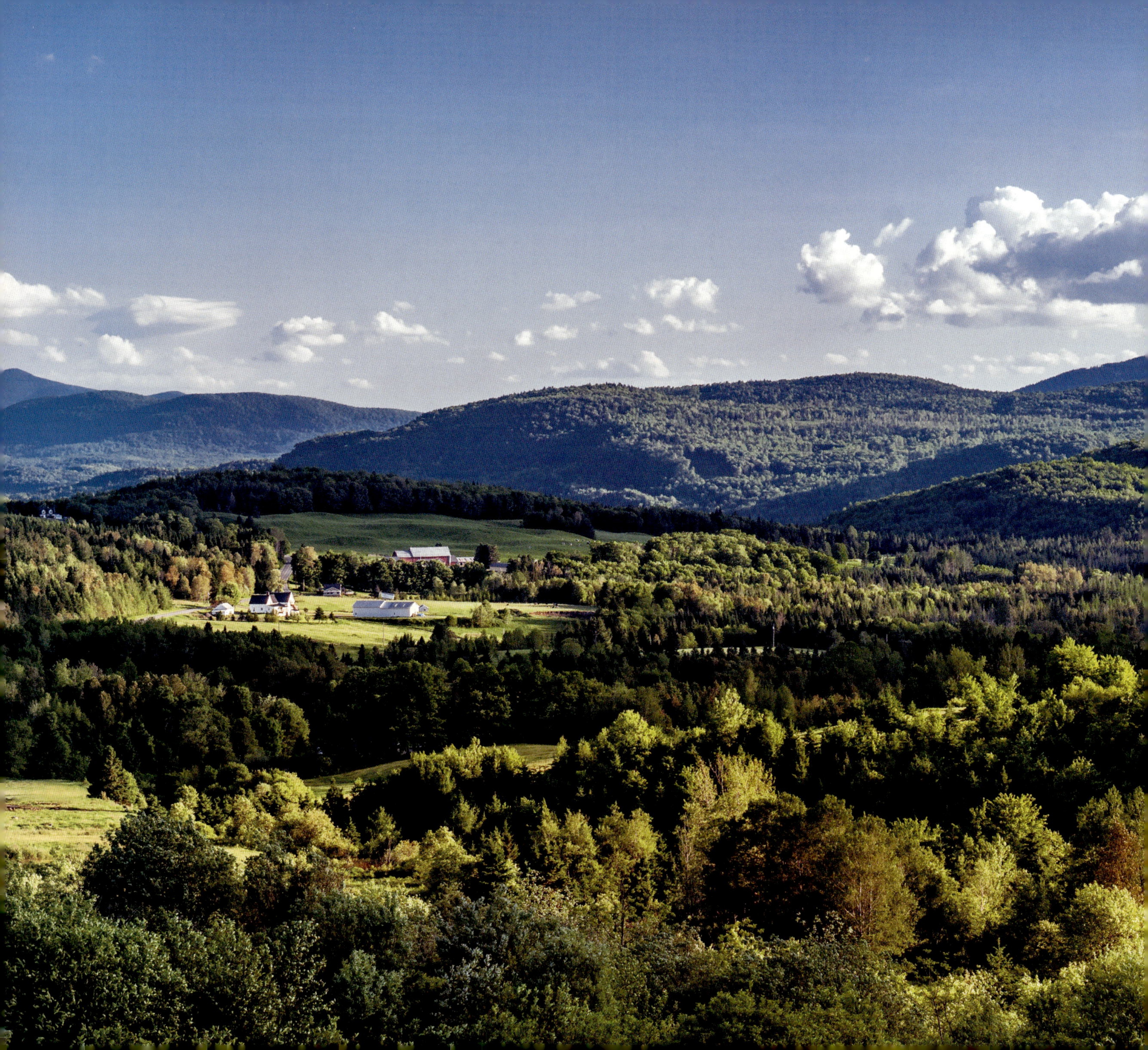

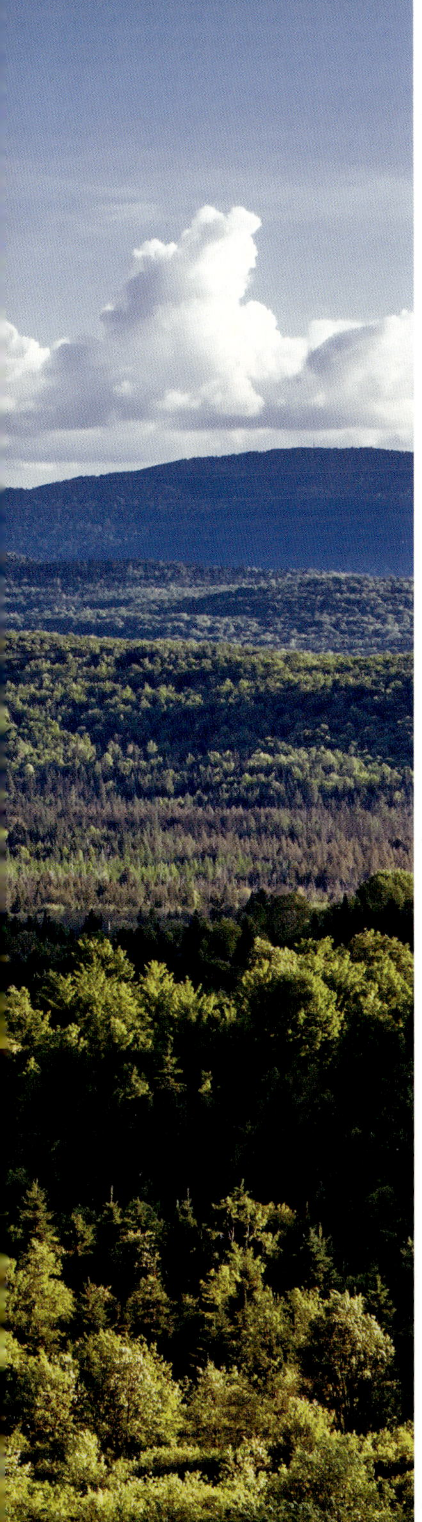

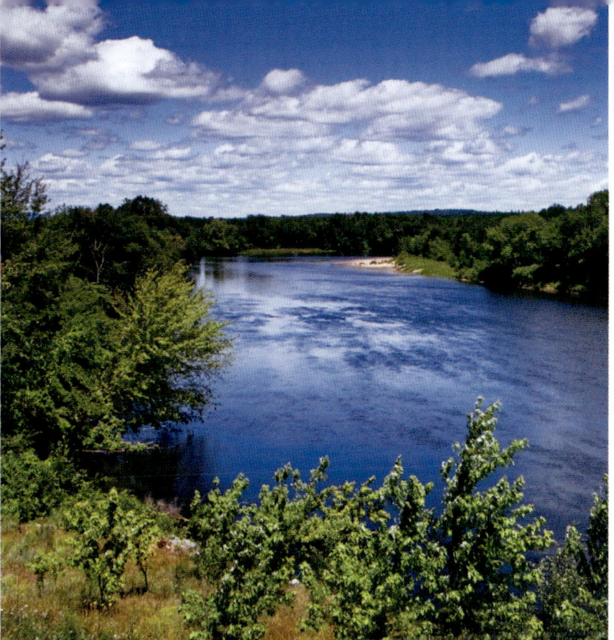

Left: A lazy Merrimack River unwinds through Boscawen on its way to the Atlantic Ocean. Its 116 miles provide ample opportunities to enjoy a tranquil paddle.

Far left: Rolling hills meet rolling farmland, and distant farmhouses are the only mark on the landscape around rural Clarksville, a small community—population 265 —near the Canadian border.

Below: It's summertime, and the living is easy on warm rocks at Five Finger Point, a scenic peninsula on Squam Lake in Sandwich, tucked away in the Lakes Region.

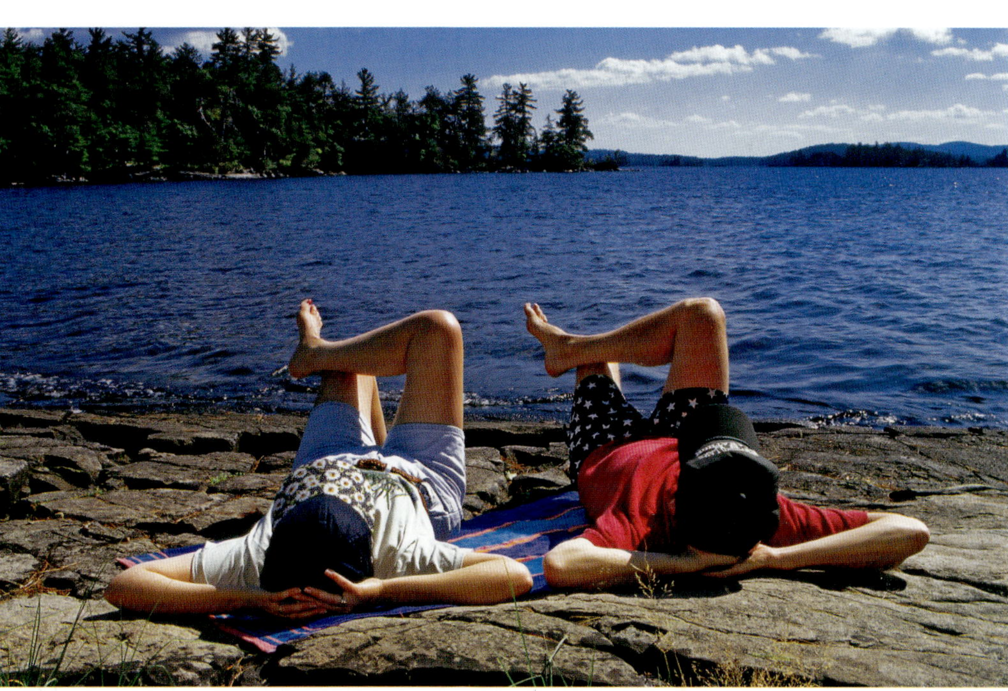

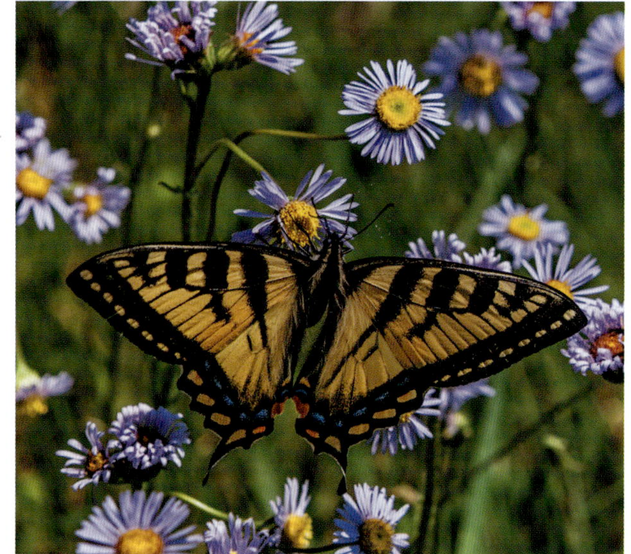

Right: A delicate eastern tiger swallowtail inspects the petals on common fleabane. The state's official butterfly is the Karner blue, found in isolated colonies in New Hampshire.

Far right: Water rushes over rock in Woodstock, not far from Franconia Notch State Park.

Below: The Connecticut River flows past Lyme, founded in 1761. The largest river in New England, it was named an American Heritage River in 1997.

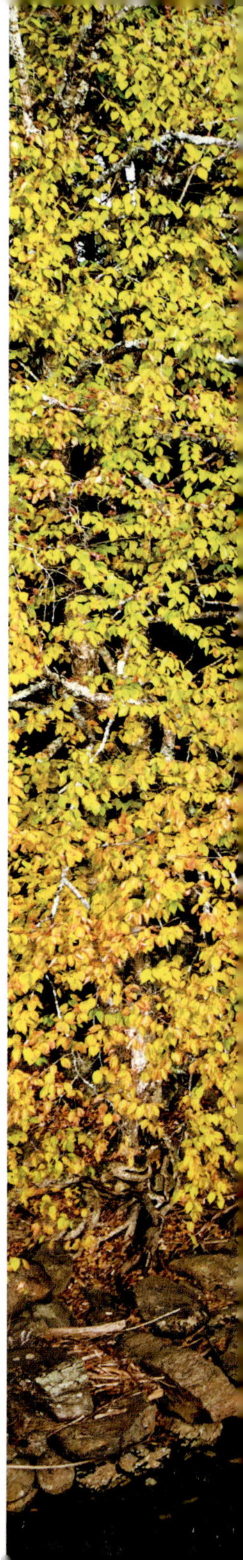

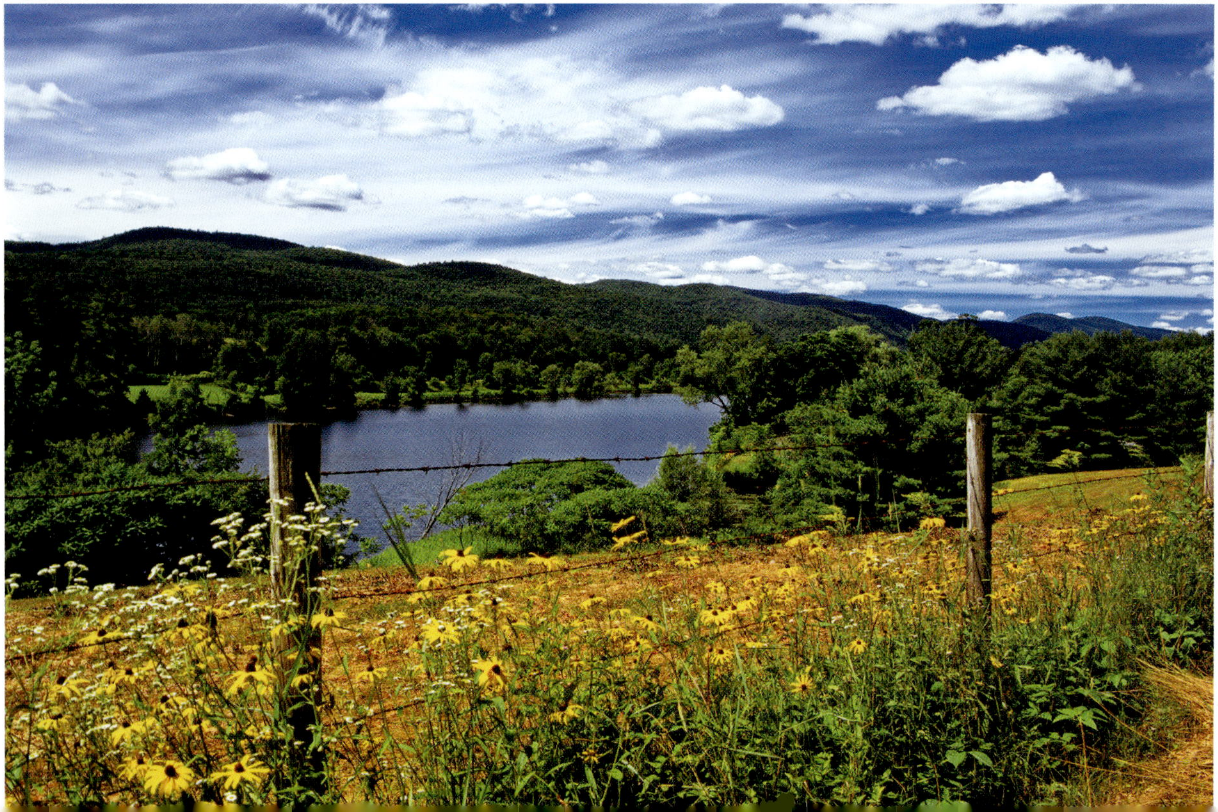

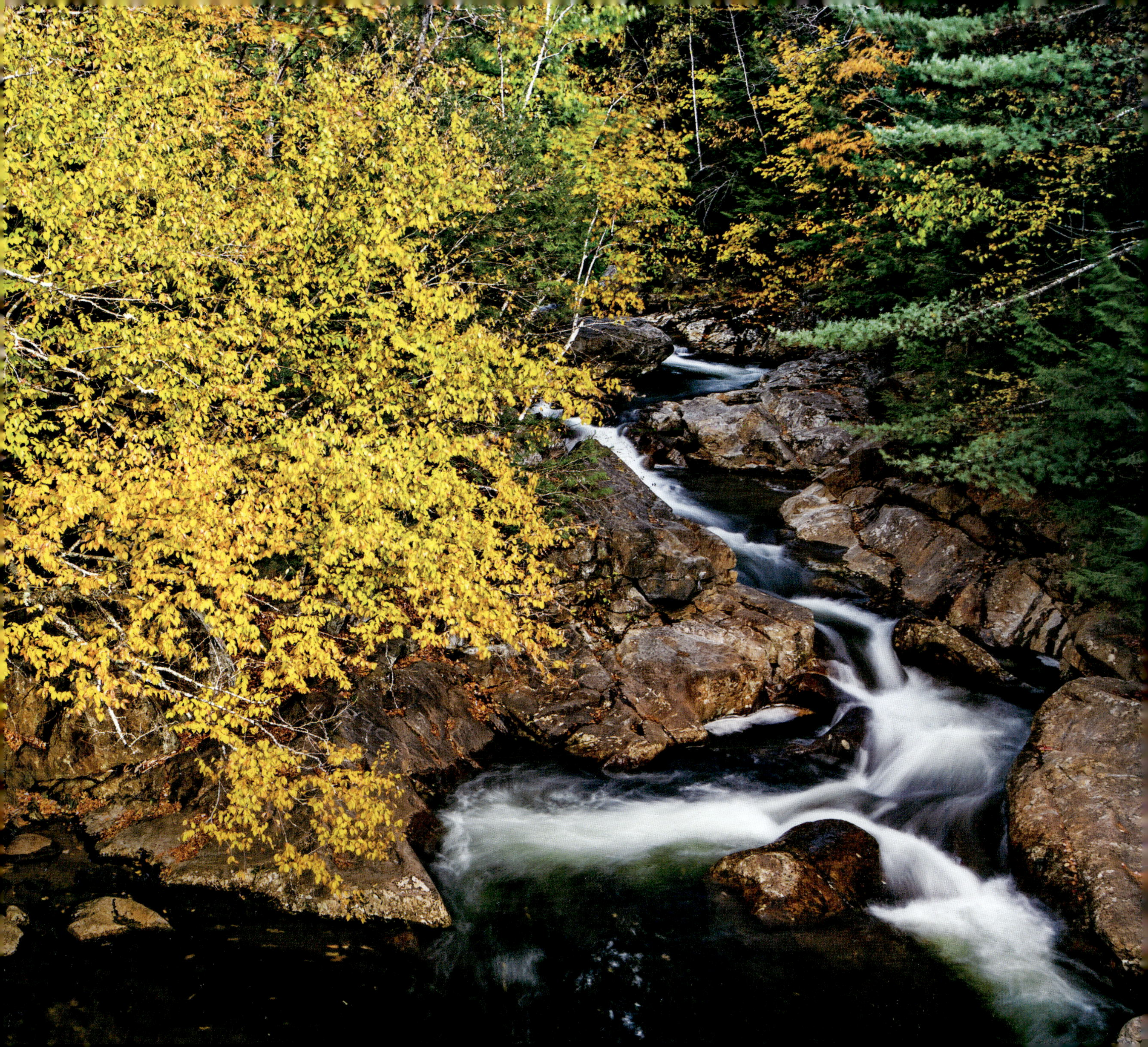

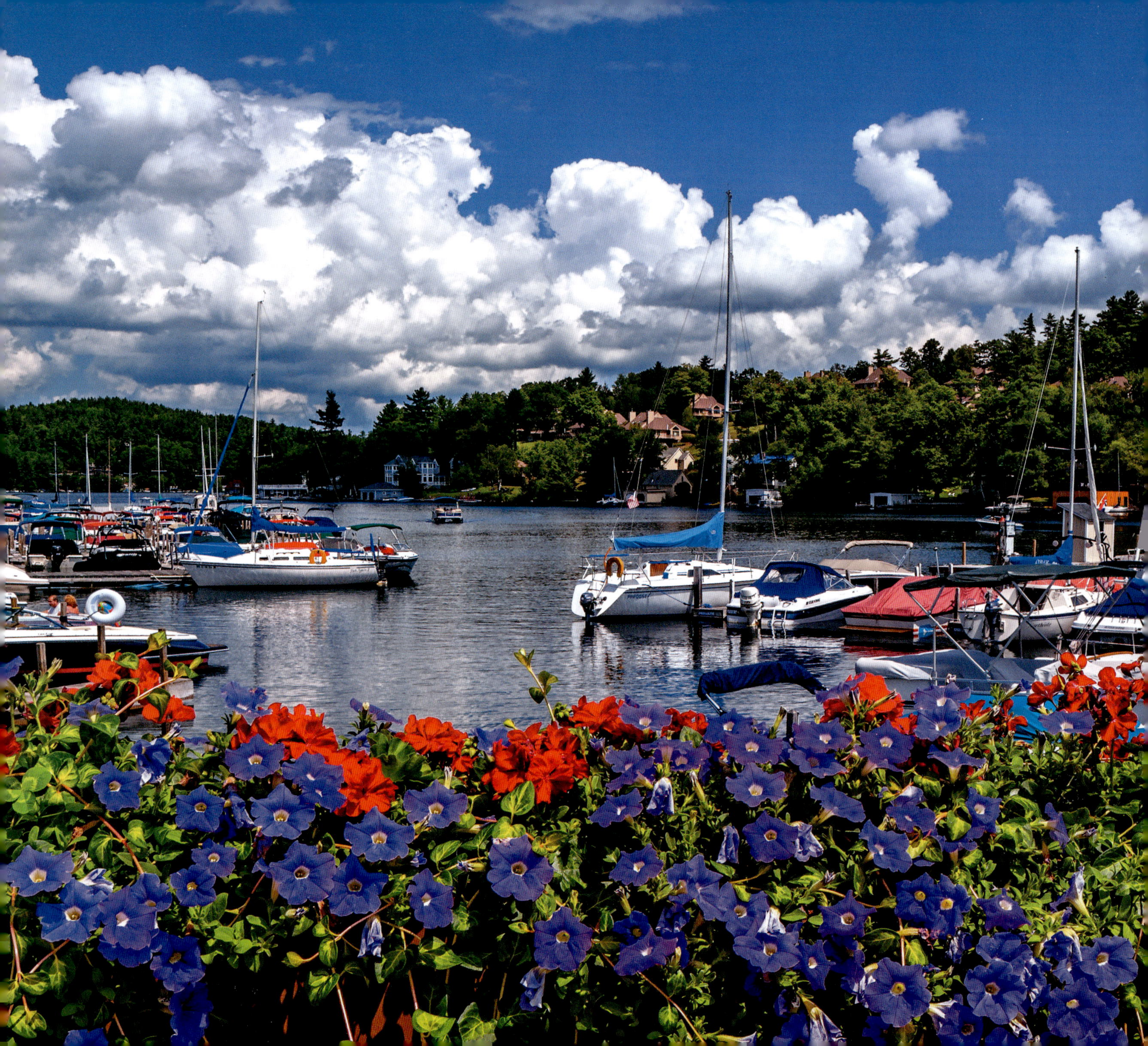

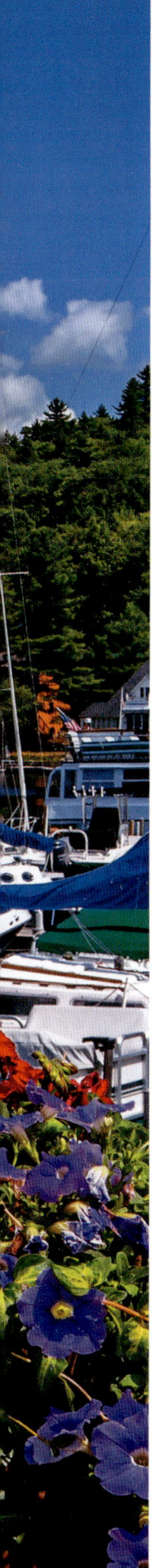

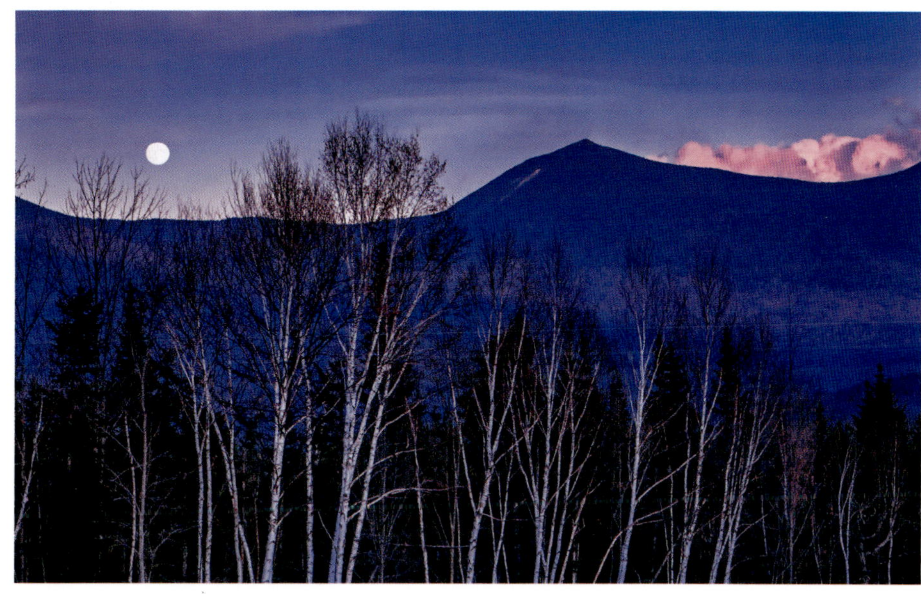

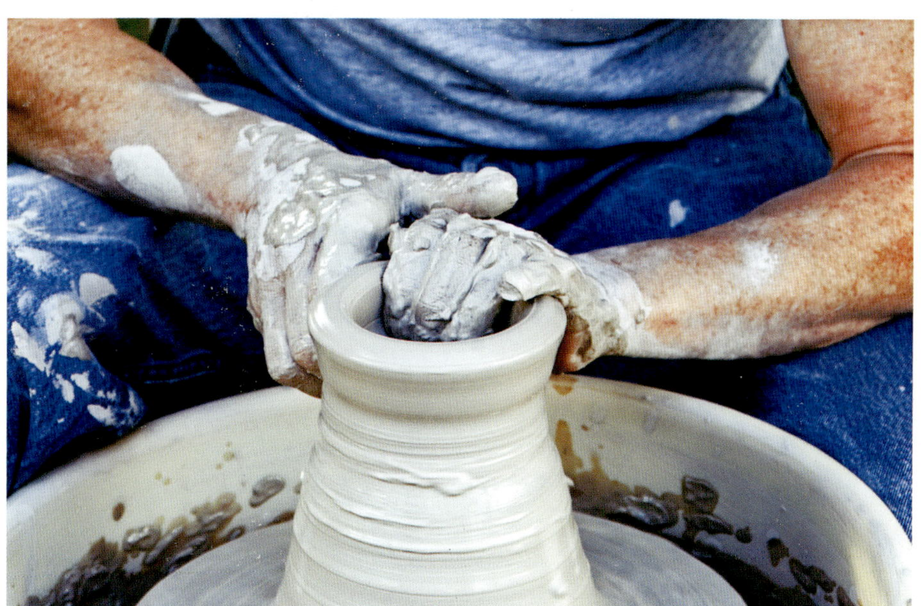

Above left: Moonrise over the White Mountains dusts a grove of bare-branched white birches, the state's official tree. A native species, its bark was once used for medicine and birch-bark canoes.

Left: Fine arts and traditional crafts are practiced throughout the state; in Newbury a skilled potter pulls form from a lump of clay at the League of New Hampshire Craftsmen fair, the nation's oldest annual craft fair.

Far left: A riot of summer petunias crowds the shore at Lake Sunapee. The harbor comes to life in warm weather, with boat tours, art galleries, and live music alongside the sparkling waters.

Facing page: North of Lake Winnipesaukee, lovely Tamworth is renowned for its Barnstormers Theatre, a professional summer theater on Main Street that has drawn audiences since 1931.

Below right: A short distance from Mount Sunapee, cozy chairs beckon campers to Kezar Lake, which borders Wadleigh State Park. A looping seventy-five-mile trail, the Sunapee-Ragged-Kearsarge Greenway, joins the park with three other state parks.

Below left: The surreal beauty of rockweed—a sea grass that provides habitat for countless organisms in coastal New England—embellishes the Piscataqua River on its way to Portsmouth Harbor.

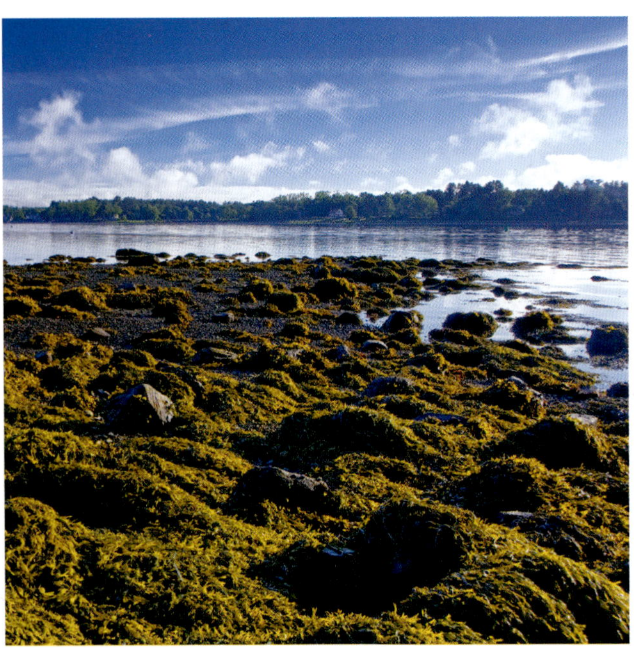

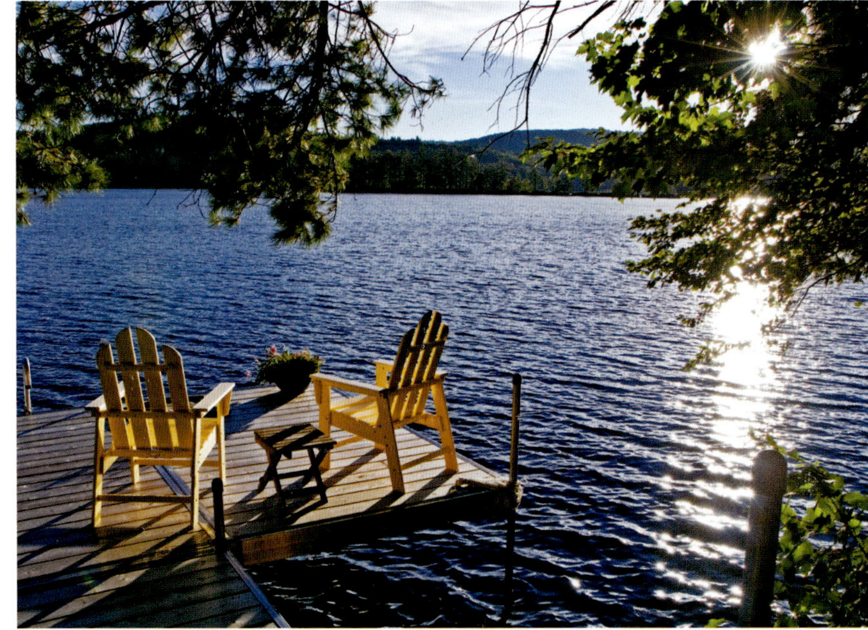

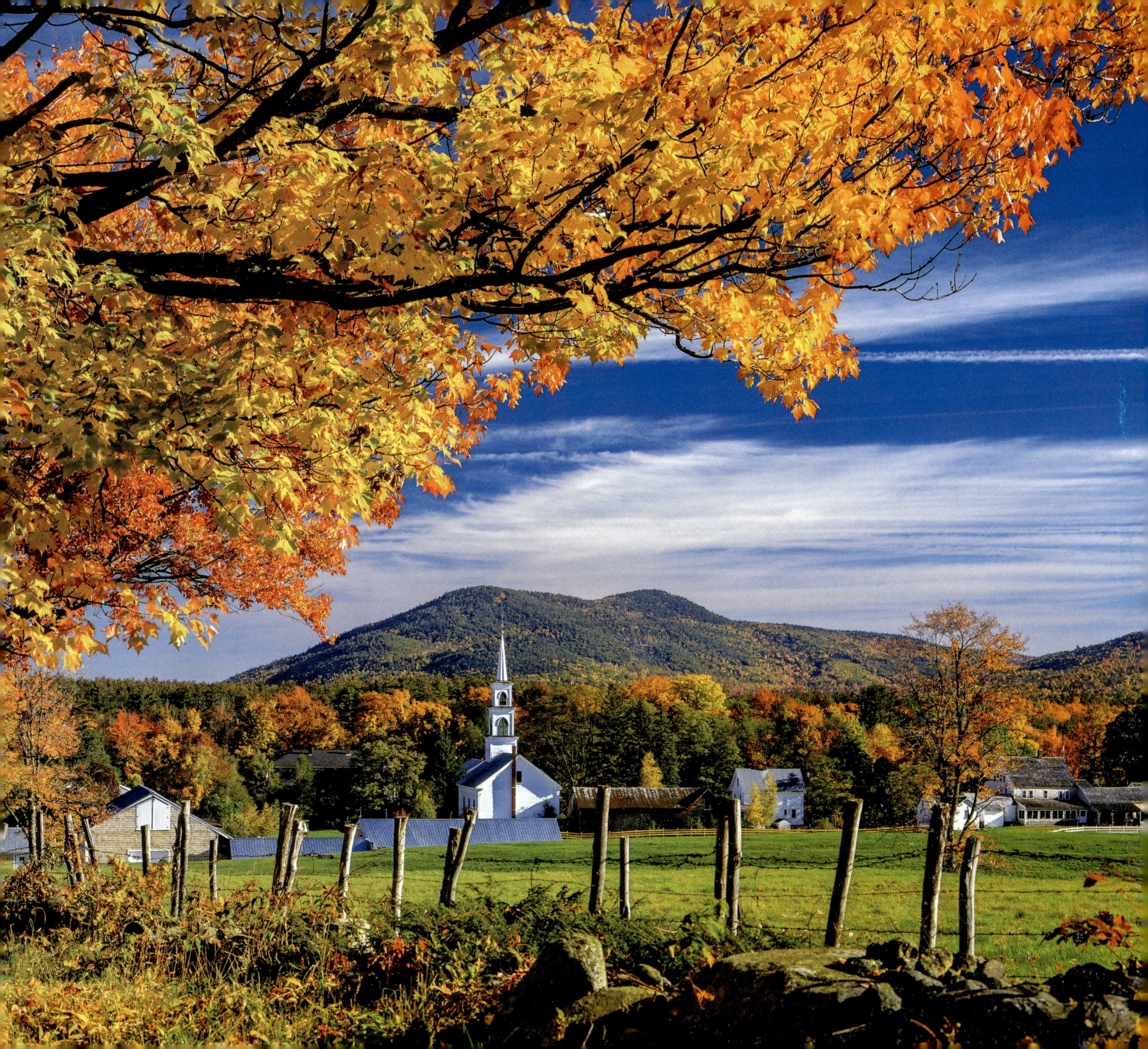

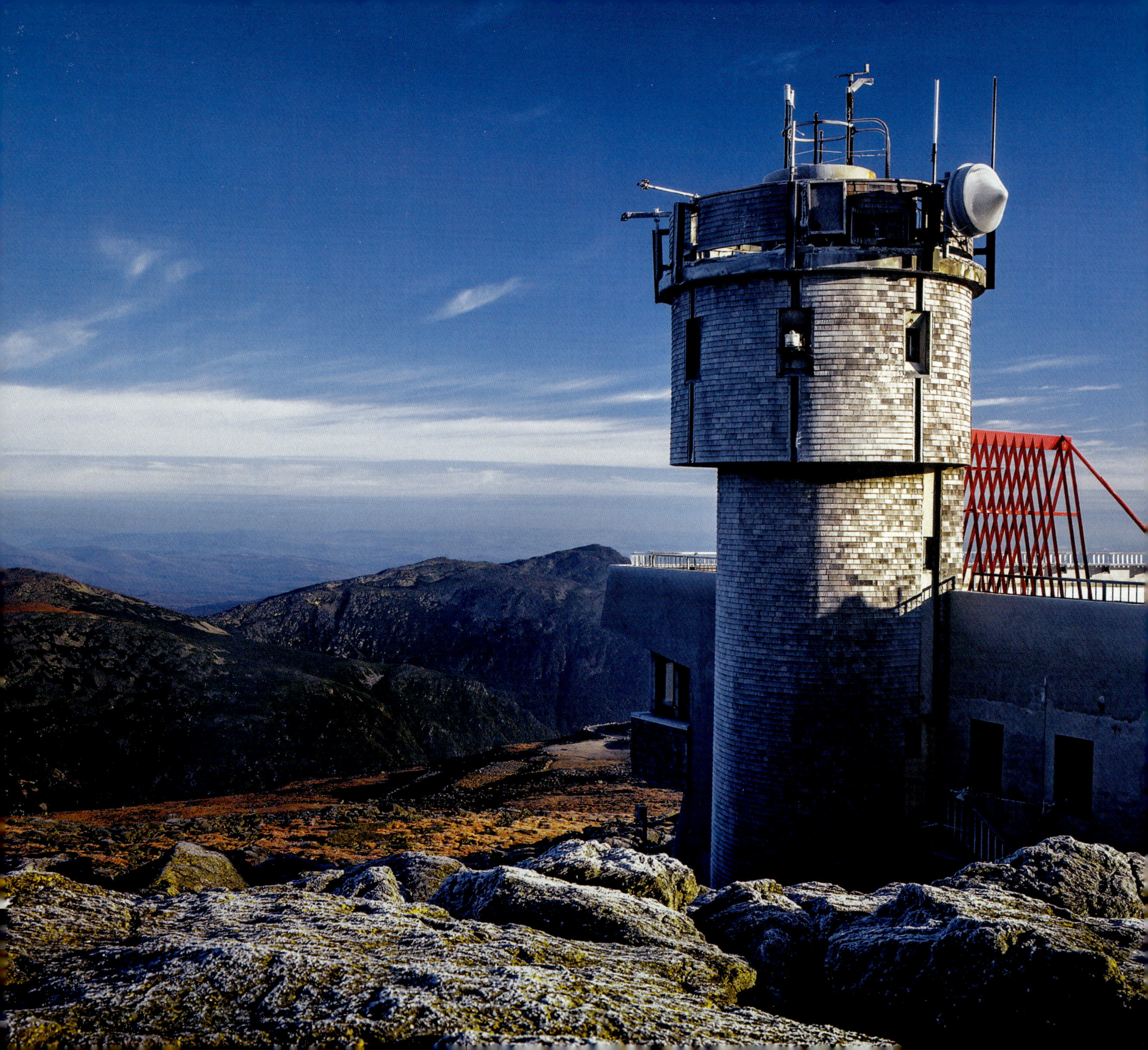

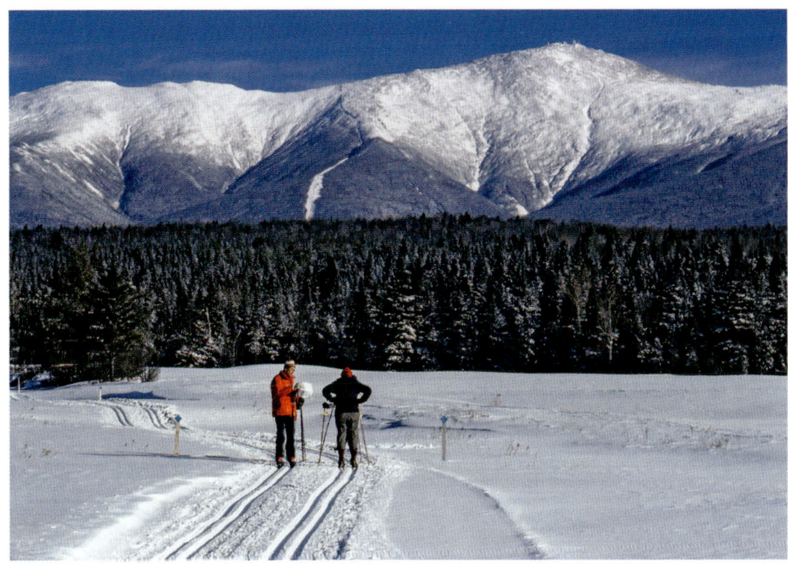

Left: Cross-country skiers at the Bretton Woods Nordic Center rest in the shadow of the snowy peaks of Mount Washington and the Presidential Range.

Facing page: The Mount Washington Observatory, atop Mount Washington, sees some of the world's most severe weather. Wind speeds and temperatures at the summit are brutal, and the research station has its own Avalanche Center. It is a go-to resource for updates on conditions at fabled Tuckerman's Ravine, the home of extreme skiing.

Below: Cairns mark the path in Mount Washington State Park. Accessible by train, road, and shuttle, the summit features hiking trails, a visitor center, and the historic Tip Top House.

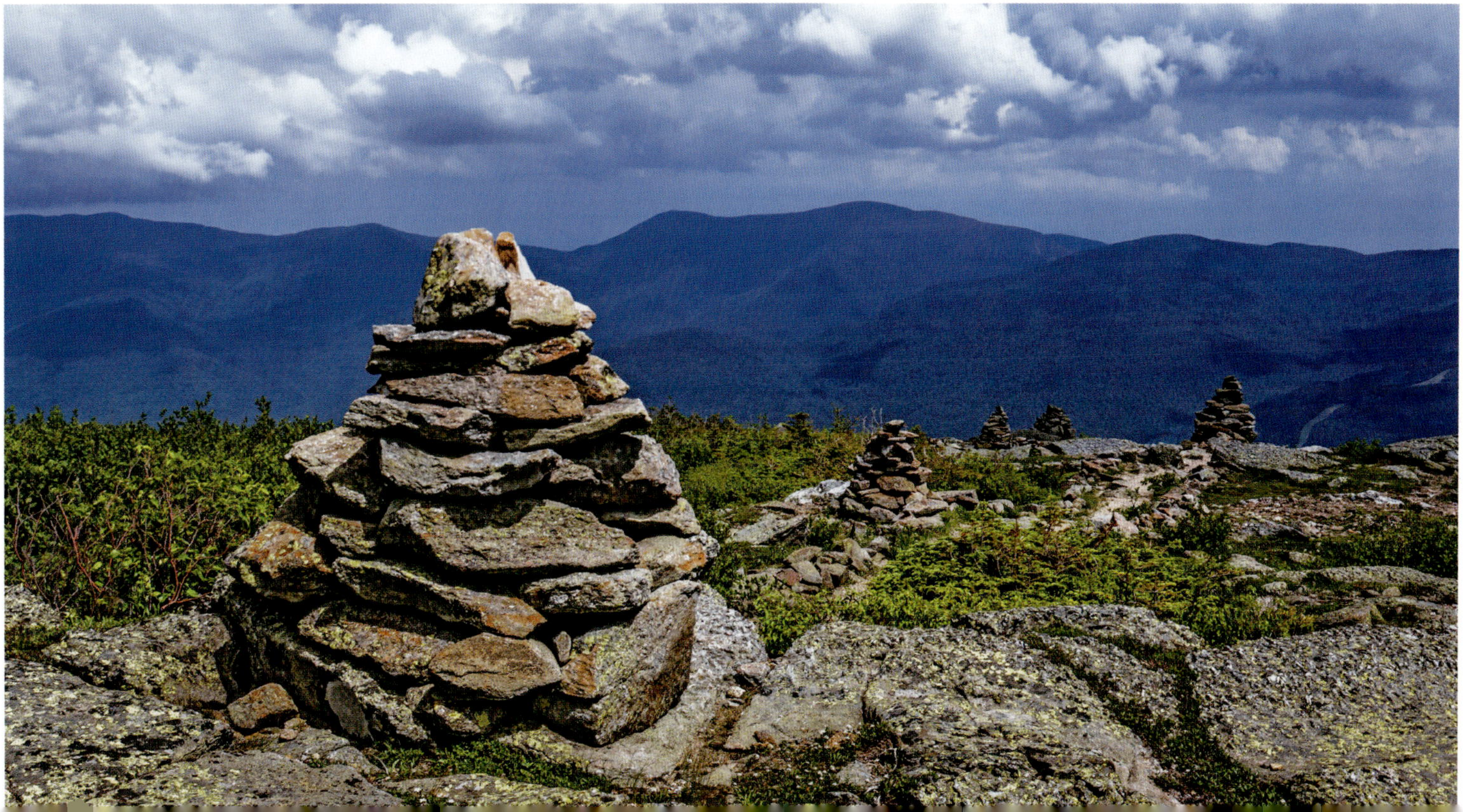

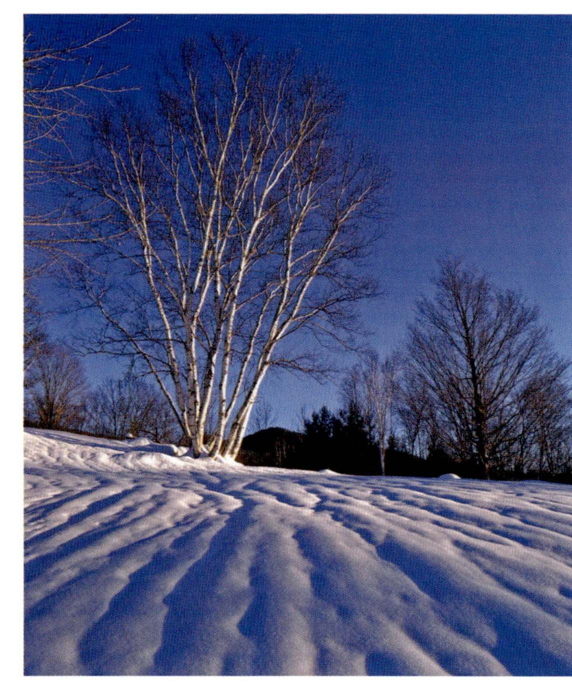

Right: Birches rise from the snow in Jackson, where Nordic skiing takes over the town in winter, crisscrossing the landscape with ski trails.

Far right: Delicate ice crystals shatter the surface of Newfound Lake at first light. Residents of this seven-mile-long Lakes Region beauty take pride in the lake's depth and spring-fed purity.

Below: The drama of a winter sky is reflected in Beaver Pond, found in the Ossipee Mountains between Tamworth and Moultonborough.

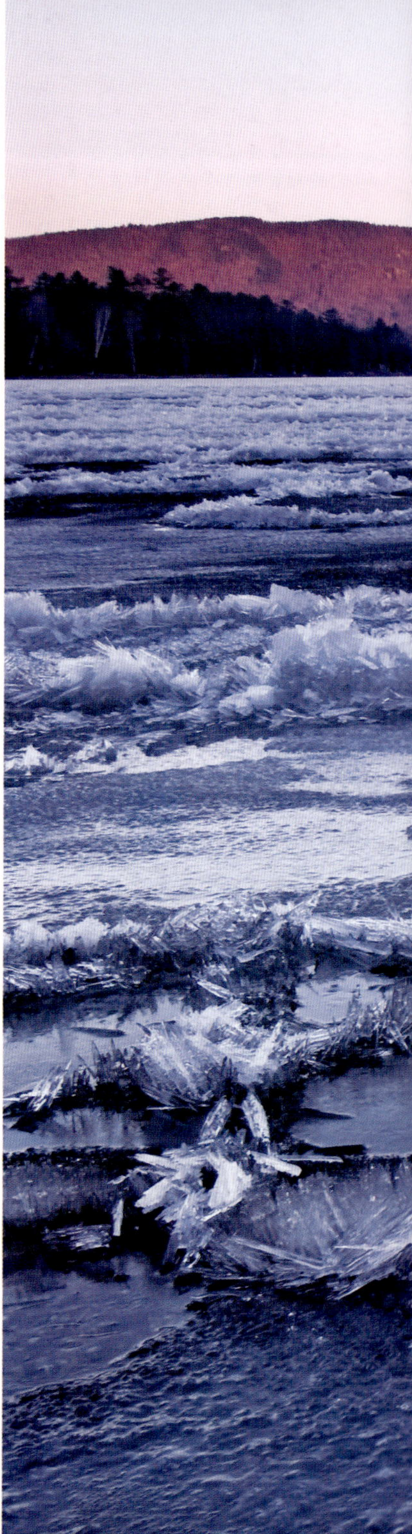

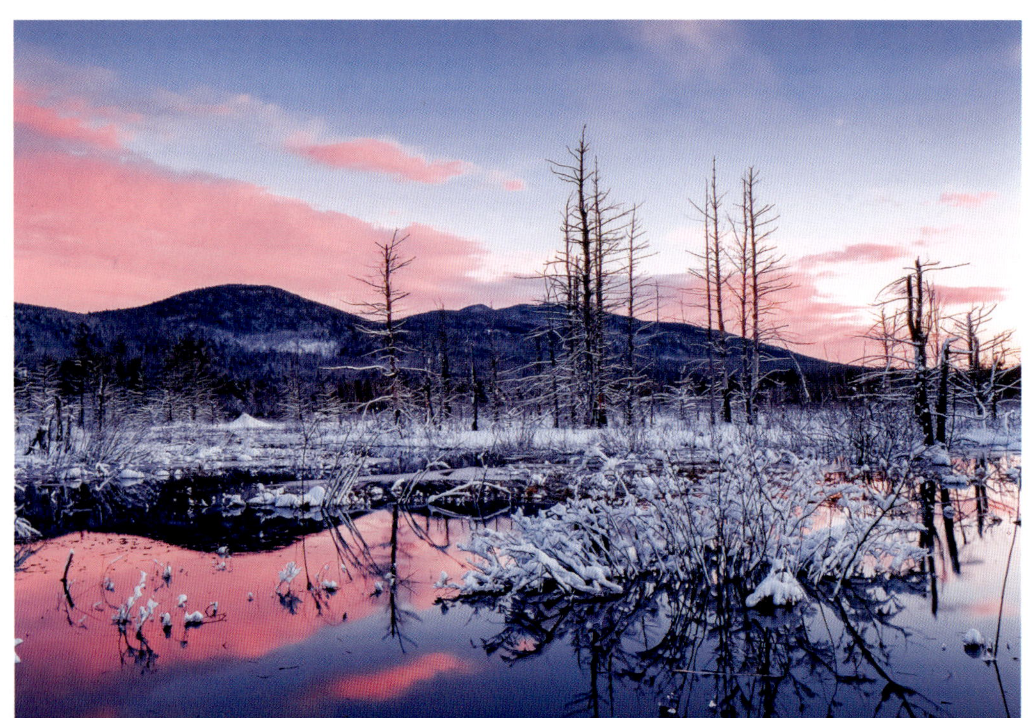

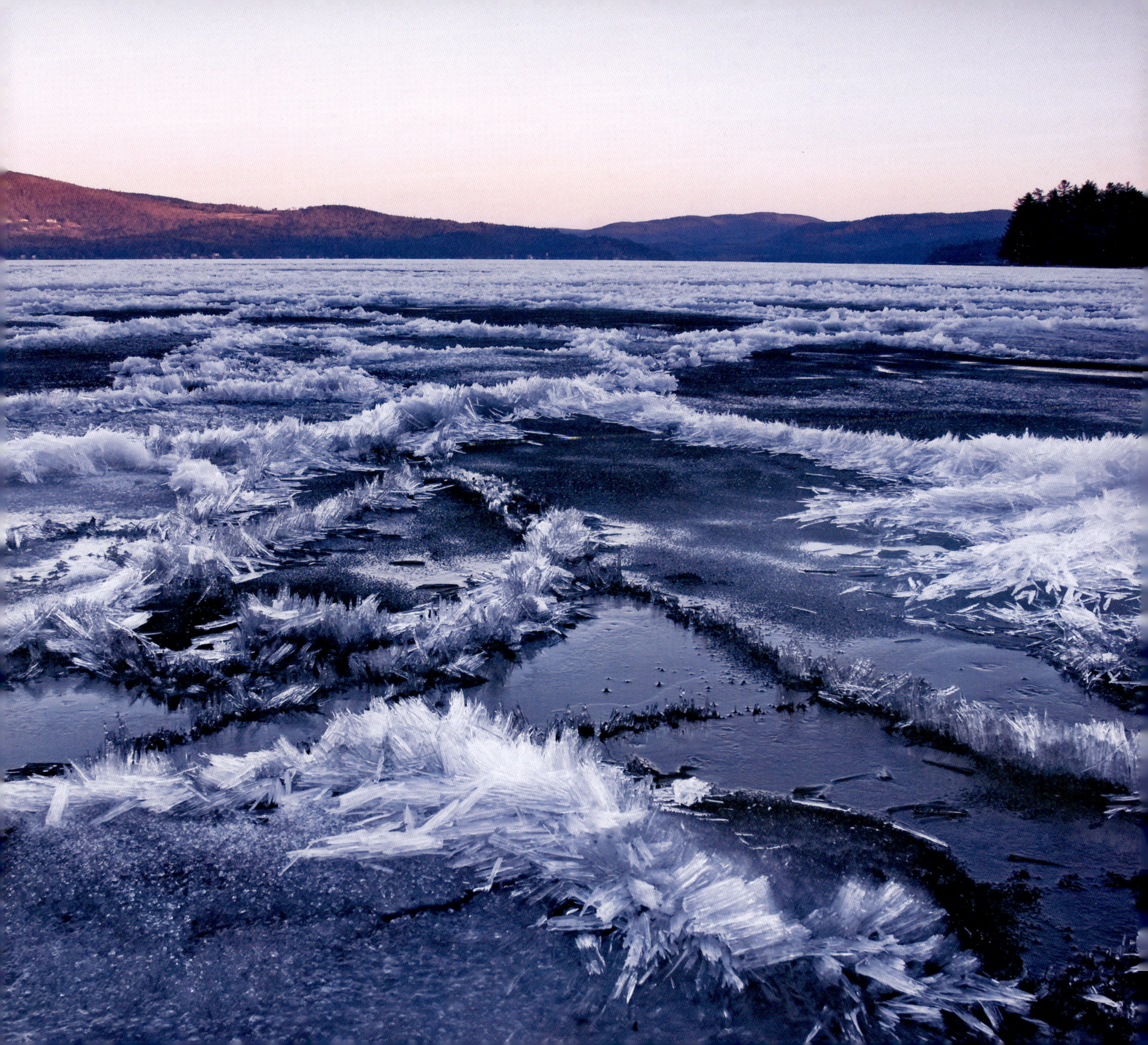

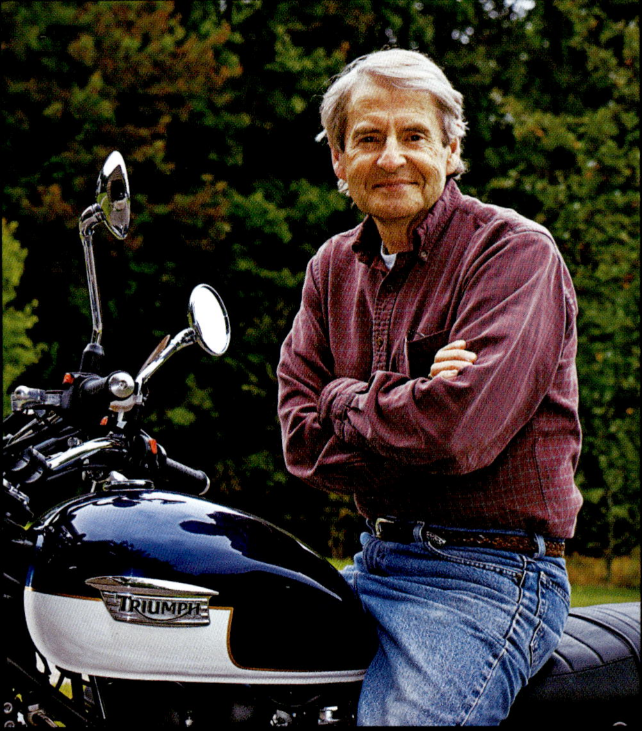

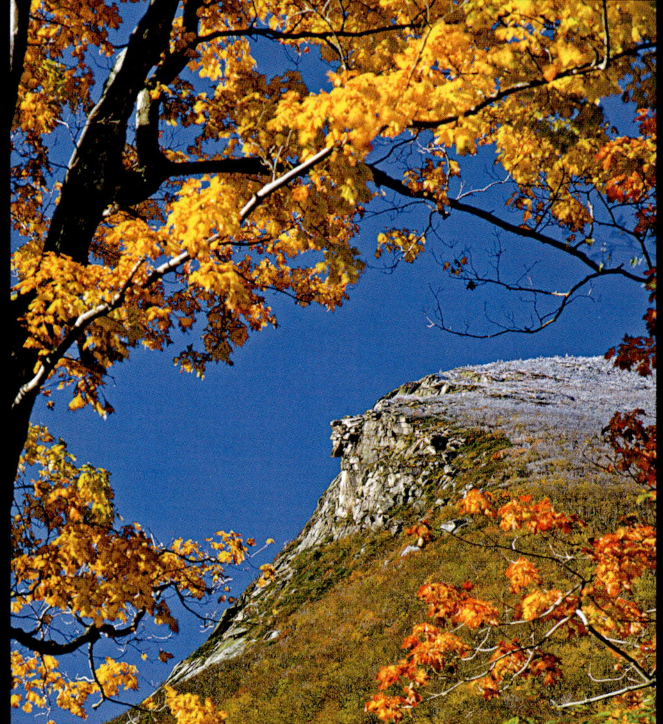

Beloved symbol of New Hampshire, the rugged rock formation Old Man of the Mountain slipped into state history in 2003, when it crumbled from the hillside at Franconia Notch State Park. The Profile Plaza, which uses granite slabs to recreate the profile, remains a popular interpretive stop at the park.

William H. Johnson

Throughout his four decades as a photographer, William H. Johnson has worked to capture the countryside of his native New England in all seasons and angles. From close-up details to sweeping landscapes, Johnson uses the natural lighting and weather conditions to capture the spirit of a place. Johnson's remarkable photography truly transports the viewer into the scene.

Johnson's work has appeared in guidebooks, calendars, postcards, greeting cards, and advertisements, and he has published in numerous magazines and newspapers, including *National Geographic Traveler, Travel + Leisure, Adventure Travel, The New York Times, Country Magazine, Yankee Magazine,* and *Vermont Life.* This is the seventh book featuring his photography.